SOUTHERN TONGUE

A Dictionary of Southern Expressions

SOUTHERN TONGUE

A Dictionary of Southern Expressions

Damon Bonds

NOMAD PUBLISHING

Southern Tongue : A Dictionary of Southern Expressions

Copyright © 2001 by Damon Bonds

For information address NOMAD PUBLISHING, P.O.Box 244722, Anchorage, AK 99524-4722

Printed and bound in the United States of America.

Publisher's Cataloging-in-Publication
(*provided by Quality Books, Inc.*)

Southern tongue : a dictionary of Southern expressions / Damon Bonds. — 1st ed.
  p. cm.
  LCCN: 00-192748
  ISBN: 0-9704671-3-3

  1. English language—Dialects—Southern States—Terms and phrases. 2. Popular culture—Southern States—Dictionaries. 3. Americanisms—Southern States—Dictionaries. I. Title.

PE2926.B66 2001   427'.975'03
                         QBI01-200876

For my family,
and anyone who misses someone.

Preface

The way I figure it, Southern dialect is as much a noteworthy part of Southern culture as corn bread and crawfish, hillbillies and honky tonks, or even, dare I say, Lynyrd Skynyrd. Southerners take great pride in their powers of expression and most would be delighted to spend an afternoon tellin' you all about it. Yep, armed with a slew of "y'all"s and "yonder"s, as well as the ever-present drawl, the Southern tongue is indeed a force to be reckoned with.

Yet, as I mosey on down the road of life, I occasionally cross paths with those who are not quite so familiar with this lingo that we Southerners hold so dear. I often find myself being questioned as to just what the hell I'm talkin' about. Other times these strange people know exactly what I'm talkin' about, but instead find great humor in mockin' my Southern manner of speakin'. ("Whar yew frum, boy? Heh, heh.")

I reckon enough attention has been called to the silly things that we say to justify a reference guide to our beautifully descriptive and often humorously twisted brand of colloquialisms; a reference for those not fortunate enough to have been born in the South and a testament to those who were. This book is my best attempt to create such a thing, in effort to present and preserve the Southern tongue, and hopefully it will serve to learn y'all just what the hell we're talkin' about.

Damon Bonds
Houston, Texas

Thank You Much:

Courtney Bonds, David Bonds, Debbie Bonds,
Neva Bonds, Ronald Bonds, Toby Boothe,
Chris Elliot, Danielle Gilbert, Jessica Guerrero,
Ed Hidlebaugh, Lisa Hidlebaugh,
Pam Hidlebaugh, Russell Hughes, Larry Kaniut,
Drew Kidwell, Brenda Laird, Elizabeth Laird,
James "Bug" Laird, Mike Ledbetter,
Bethany Lee, Aaron Madole, Jason McCaleb,
the late Reba McKenzie, Billy Moore,
Gloria Morris, Paul Netherland, Josh Pershall,
Shirley Shofner, Jim Stevens, Tom Swarthout,
Len Vaughn, Lenard Vaughn, Linda Vaughn,
J. D. Webb, Jim West, Kevin West,
and Dan Wright

Introduction

Southern Tongue is a compilation of words, expressions, colloquialisms, and proverbs common to the Southern United States. Much of the information presented here was donated by bonified Southerners who were asked to provide expressions commonly used in their daily communication, but that might not be so common outside of the South; expressions that they felt were quintessentially Southern. As such, this is a book written by the South, about the South. It allows us to see the South as the South sees itself. It gives us a greater look at the expressions in current use and living memory rather than outdated literary lingo and civil war terms.

The purpose of this book is to provide a reference tool to the language of the South for those who might not readily understand it. It exists to entertain the Southerner and to educate the non-Southerner. More than that it is simply a gift to the South, to stand as a monument to our ancestors and to be passed along to our children.

This collection is a large part of who we are; colorful and creative, ornery and original. This book would not exist if not for the hospitality, inspiration, and support of many proud Southerners who endeavor to keep the American culture diverse by continuing to use these flavorful expressions. We hope you enjoy reading this book as much as we enjoy *being* it.

Disclaimer

Southern lingo, however unique, is merely a thread of the American fabric. Dialects across America have blended over decades, and some once regional expressions are now heard nationwide. "Come hell or high water", for example, is commonplace across the United States and "pert near" has been uttered by people from such strange places as New York City. Likewise, expressions from elsewhere have been assimilated and made our own by collective use, alternate pronunciation, and regional connotations. As such, no claim is made that all entries are exclusively Southern or necessarily of Southern origin; however, these words and expressions "hit home" with enough Southerners to be included and most entries were submitted via "the grapevine" by the South's finest.

Please note that some of the expressions herein may be considered distasteful in certain circles, but were included due to the fact that they exist. The use of these "questionable" words is strongly discouraged and where they occur in the following text, a reminder of the offensive nature of the word has been given in lieu of a sample sentence. In addition, the Confederate flag is currently under attack; however, it was ultimately selected for the cover of this book as it remains the number one icon of the South. For the purposes of this book, the flag represents the South and Southern culture, in common, and nothing more.

~A~

a---used before any verb, pronounced "uh"

I'm a goin' a fishin' come Sun-up.

aback of---behind

If yer lookin' fer Daddy, he's aback of the house mowin' the yard.

a coon's age---
a very long time

I haven't seen you in a coon's age! How have you been?

actin' up---1) hurting, ailing

Granny cain't walk too fast on account of her knees are actin' up.

2) misbehaving

You kids are gonna get a whippin' if y'all don't quit actin' up!

addled---confused

These crossword puzzles get me plum addled.

a doin'---a happening, an event

There's a doin' up at the fair grounds this weekend. It must be time for the annual chili cook-off.

a far cry from---
incomparable to;
of lesser quality

I've got a nice house, but it's a far cry from the Playboy mansion.

afeared---afraid, scared

I ain't afeared of the dark, Momma, but will you leave the hall light on anyway?

afore---before

You best come inside afore you catch a cold.

agin'---against

Don't lean agin' the car. You might scratch it.

a good bit---a substantial amount

We got a pretty good bit of rain yesterday.

a great while---a long time

I haven't seen you in a great while.

a hair---a small increment; a little bit

Could you scoot over a hair and give me some elbow room?

aholt---1) a hold, a grasp

Grab aholt of the rope and I'll pull you up.

2) in contact with

Whar you been? I've been tryin' to get aholt of you all day.

aig---a common pronunciation of "egg"

Go out to the chicken coop and fetch some aigs fer breakfast.

aim to/aimin' to---
to have intent to do

I aim to kill me a deer by sundown.

ain't---1) am not, are not, is not

Robert: *You ain't from around here, are ya?*
Ellen: *No, I ain't.*

2) have not

I ain't seen you in ages.

3) a common pronunciation of "aunt"

ain't got no---"have no"

I ain't got no extra money.

ain't got none (of them thar)---"don't have any (of those)"

Customer: *Ain't ya got none of them thar moon pies?*
Clerk: *Nope. I ain't got none.*

ain't much to look at---unattractive; displeasing to the eye

This ol' truck ain't much to look at, but she's real dependable.

ain't never---have not ever

I ain't never been to the big city.

ain't no skin off my ass---"It doesn't affect or bother me"

Husband: *Do you mind if I go out bowlin' with the boys tonight?*
Wife: *Ain't no skin off my ass. Tonight's my bridge night anyhow.*

ain't seen much of---have not encountered

I ain't seen much of him since he moved to Memphis.

aintser---pronunciation of "answer"

They should put me on Jeopardy. I know all the aintsers.

air up---to inflate

I need to stop by the gas station and air up my tires.

akin---related

Paw says we're akin to half the population of Louisiana.

all bark and no bite---"all talk and no action"

Just ignore him. He's all bark and no bite.

all hat and no cattle---"all image"; said of those who portray themselves as something they are not; (see "all bark and no bite")

She struts around like she's the belle of the ball, but I think she's all hat and no cattle.

alligator pear---an avocado

I never have really liked alligator pears.

all she wrote---an end to something

We were fixin' to set that cat on fire, but mama caught us, and that was all she wrote.

all vine and no taters---(see "all bark and no bite")

Don't worry, my dog won't bite you. She sounds viscous but she's all vine and no taters.

a load of corn---a lie

She acts like she's poor, but that's a load a corn.

alright then---o.k., agreed

Ma: *I'll go get the movies if you'll go get the beer.* Pa: *Alright then.*

alrighty---o.k., agreed

Joe: *I'll pick you up at 6:00.* Courtney: *Alrighty. I'll be waitin' fer ya.*

a mite---a fair amount

I feel a mite tired. I reckon I'm due for some shut-eye.

animule---animal

Paw, can we go to the zoo and see the animules?

antsy---restless, hyper, anxious

You're awful antsy. How many cups of coffee have you had today?

any further than one can throw---none at all

I don't trust him any further than I can throw him.

anyhow---anyway

I missed the bus, but I didn't really want to go, anyhow.

anymore---nowadays, currently

Anymore, it's all I can do just to get up and go to work.

anywho---anyhow

Anywho, I gotta go now.

a piece---a short distance

There's a creek with a nice swimmin' hole just up the road a piece.

a plenty---plenty, enough, a large amount

You shouldn't come visit in summer lessen you like mosquitoes a plenty.

Appalachians---a mountain range common to many Southern states

I broke my leg hiking in the Appalachians.

apple picker--- a "pooper scooper" for horses

The worst job I ever had was following a parade with an apple picker.

Arkansas toothpick--- 1) a Bowie knife; any large knife

I once saw a man cut another man from ear to ear with an Arkansas toothpick.

2) the bone in a raccoon's penis, sold as a novelty toothpick

You can buy an Arkansas Toothpick at any Southern truckstop.

Arkie---a person born, raised, or living in Arkansas

I've got a friend who married an Arkie. Now they're livin' somewhere in the Ozarks.

ary---any

I bought three new guns, but I ain't had a chance to shoot ary of them.

a sight for sore eyes--- someone beautiful to behold; a compliment

Well, aren't you a sight for sore eyes! You're sure to win the beauty contest.

**as much chance as a
one-legged man at an
ass-kickin' contest**---
no chance at all

*I don't think she'd ever
go out with me. I've got
about as much chance as
a one-legged man at an
ass-kickin' contest.*

ass end---rear end; back
side

*I backed into a tree and tore
up the ass end of my truck.*

ass whippin'---physical
punishment; a spanking;
a beating

*That dog's gonna get an
ass whippin' next time I
catch him chewin' on my
shoes!*

as the crow flies---
distance in a straight
line between two points,
as opposed to a longer
route

*It's only thirty miles to
Grandma's house as the
crow flies, but I like to
take the back roads.*

as the day is long---
expression adding
emphasis to the point
being made

*That Chihuahua is as ugly
as the day is long.*

**as welcome as a skunk at
a lawn party**---
positively not welcome

*I think you should leave
now. You're about as
welcome around here as
a skunk at a lawn party.*

'at---common pronunciation
of "that"

*'At's got to be the laziest
dog I ever did see.*

a talkin' to---a lecture; verbal punishment

I gave that boy a good talkin' to, but I don't think it did a bit of good.

a'tall---at all

I broke my toe, but it didn't hurt a'tall.

ate supper before they said Grace---said of couples having sex before marriage

Them two ought to be ashamed of themselves. You know they ate supper before they said Grace.

ate up---infected

I can't make it to work today on account of I'm ate up with the flu.

ate up with the dumbasses---to lack focus, to be clumsy or foolish

I lost my wallet, locked my keys in the car, and stubbed my toe. I think I'm ate up with the dumbasses.

attaboy/attagirl--- common praise

Attaboy! I knew you could do it!

a ways---a moderate distance

We're gettin' closer, but Grandma's house is still a ways away.

awful---very, excessively

You need to stay in bed. You're awful sick.

a whole nuther---another, separate from

...but now that's a whole nuther story altogether.

awrite---"all right"; in response to "How are you?", used as a greeting to save the other person from having to ask

Boudreaux: *Awrite.*
Broussard: *Awrite.*

axe to grind---a dispute to address; a problem to discuss

I've got an axe to grind with that boy. He ain't showed up for work all week.

~B~

backasswards/
bassackwards---
backwards

I wonder if that feller knows he's got his shirt on backasswards?

back in the day---"when times were better"; long ago

Back in the day, I could box with the best of 'em.

backwoods---1) residing or raised in the woods; implies ignorance or low social standing

My daughter decided to marry some backwoods moron.

2) deep forest, far from civilization

We got lost in the backwoods and it took us three days to find a road.

bad blood---ill feelings, hatred

My in-laws hate me. There's years of bad blood between us.

bad mouth---to insult or speak negatively of someone or something

Don't you be bad mouthin' my cookin'. I'll whup you good!

bad off---in bad shape, not well

Bubba got hit by a car and now he's pretty bad off.

Bama/Bamy---the state of Alabama

Uncle Pete once shot a man down in Bamy.

banjo---a stringed instrument common in the South

I used to play the banjo when I was a kid. Nothin' like sittin' around with yer friends, a pickin' and a grinnin'.

banquette---sidewalk (Cajun)

You know you had a good time in New Orleans when you find yourself throwin' up on the banquette at four in the mornin'.

bar---a common pronunciation of "bear"

I seen a bar out back last week. So be careful out there!

bar-B-Q---barbecue; a "get together" where barbecue is cooked and served

I'm goin' to a bar-B-Q down at the park. Wanna come?

bard---a common pronunciation of "borrowed"

Damn it, Ethel! Your brother bard 20 dollars from me, 6 months ago, and he still ain't paid me back!

barking spider--- a fictitious scapegoat for an accidental expulsion of gas from the body

Ma: *Did you just fart?* Pa: *Nope. It musta been a barkin' spider.*

barking up the wrong tree---approaching the wrong person

If you're comin' to me for advice, you're barkin' up the wrong tree.

bark is worse than one's bite---insinuates that someone is "all talk and no action"

I ain't skeered of you. Your bark is worse than your bite.

barn raisin'---a gathering for the purpose of erecting a barn.

There's gonna be a barn raisin' over at Willard's place next Friday.

barrel into---to leap into, to plunge into, to run into, to collide with

Don't barrel off into the lake. You might land on a rock and hurt yourself.

barry---pronunciation of "borrow"

Can I barry a cup of sugar?

bayou---a narrow "finger" of a larger body of water

You should've seen the size of the fish I caught down at the bayou.

beautimous---beautiful; excellent

That sunset is absolutely beautimous!

beat with an ugly stick---to be extremely physically unattractive

Damn! Someone must've beat her with an ugly stick!

beat/kick the tar/fire---to pummel excessively

I beat the tar outta that dog last time he chewed up my shoes.

bedpost---to confine a small child by putting his/her shirt tail under a bedpost

Children! I'll bedpost you both if y'all don't quit fightin'!

beehind---pronunciation of "behind"; buttocks

You smart off to me one more time and I'mone spank your beehind!

beer barn---a drive-through liquor store

Stop at the beer barn and pick me up a twelve-pack.

beholden---indebted

Thanks for your help. I'm forever beholden to you.

belle---a beautiful girl

My girlfriend is a real Southern belle.

belle of the ball---the prettiest girl at a social function

Don't you look beautiful! You're gonna be the belle of the ball!

bellyache---to whine or complain

Must you always bitch and bellyache when you don't get your way?

best---"better"

You best behave or I'll give you a whippin' you'll never forget!

better than a sharp stick in the eye---"better than nothing"; not as bad as it could be

Jesse: *I only won five dollars at the casino.*
Earl: *Well, that's better than a sharp stick in the eye!*

bet the farm---to wager everything

The value of that stock is rising fast, but I wouldn't bet the farm on it!

betweenst---between

He made me so mad I hauled off and punched him right betweenst the eyes.

be ugly---to be mean

Don't be ugly to your sister! That's not very nice.

bible belt---used to refer to the South as a place of strong religious belief

Watch your mouth! They won't put up with that kind of blaspheme in the bible belt.

bickerin'---1) arguing

My wife and I went to marriage counseling, but we just couldn't quit bickerin'.

2) complaining

Quit yer bickerin'. I'm tired of listenin' to it.

bigger 'n Dallas---"bigger than Dallas"; surely, definitely

My grandmother's got the luck of the Irish. Put her in front of a slot machine and, bigger 'n Dallas, she's gonna win.

big pile---a great deal

MaMa loves you big pile.

birthin'---giving birth (to)

As a male, birthin' and breast feedin' are not my areas of expertise.

bitch---the middle of a bench automobile seat as opposed to the driver's position on the left and "shotgun" on the right.

You rode shotgun on the way here so you have to ride bitch on the way back.

bite off more than one can chew---to undertake more than one can handle

I bit off more than I can chew. There's no way I'll have all this work done by my deadline.

bite one's tongue---1) to immediately regret having said something

I bit my tongue for invitin' Mildred to the show. I was just tryin' to be polite.

2) to refrain from speaking

Boy, you'll bite your tongue if you want to live to see tomorrow!

bite to eat---a meal

I shore am hungry. You wanna go get a bite to eat?

blacker than Toby's ass---extremely black or dark

That's one hell of a shiner you got there. It's blacker than Toby's ass!

black-eyed peas and rooster knees---black-eyed peas and chicken legs

Momma says we're havin' black-eyed peas and rooster knees for supper.

bleedin' like a stuck pig---bleeding profusely

I stepped on a nail and started bleedin' like a stuck pig.

bless your heart---1) an affectionate expression of pity

Ol' Bessie never was much to look at, bless her heart.

2) an expression of affection or appreciation

Grandson: *I brought you some flowers, Granny.* Granny: *Well, bless your heart! Aren't you just the sweetest thing!*

blinky---spoiled (milk)

I always check the baby's milk to make sure it hasn't gone blinky.

blood---a relative

I'd do anything for you. After all, you're blood.

blowed up---blew up

Jimmy lit a firecracker, but it blowed up in his hand before he could throw it.

blow in/blowed in/blew in---to arrive suddenly

My brother blew in last night around 7:00.

blowin' smoke---talking about doing something rather than actually doing it; lying

She says she's gonna quit her job, but I think she's just blowin' smoke.

blowin' smoke up one's ass---lying to or deceiving someone

She says she loves me, but she's just blowin' smoke up my ass.

blue as a possums cod---
a deep blue

Remember when you choked on that chicken bone? I swear your face turned as blue as a possums cod.

bluegrass---a style of free-form country music popular in the South

There's nothin' quite like that good ol' Tennessee bluegrass.

blue norther---a cold front from the arctic, void of precipitation (see "norther")

Better take your coat to school today. There's a blue norther on the way.

blues---a musical style popular in the South

You gotta pay yer dues to learn to play the blues.

bobo/booboo---juvenile lingo for a cut, a bruise, or any injury

Awww, did her fall down an' get a booboo?

bob war---a common pronunciation of "barbed wire"

I need to put up a bob war fence to keep my cows in.

bodacious---exceptional; grand

She was the most bodacious woman I've ever met!

boll weevil---a disreputable person

That no good boll weevil stole my John Deere!

bone to pick---something to confront or question someone about

Have you seen Fanny Mae? I've got a bone to pick with her.

boocoo(s)---a common pronunciation of the French "beaucoup"; a large quantity

I've got boocoos of work to get done today.

boogered up---botched, broken, blemished

I used to have a nice couch, but now it's all boogered up from the dog chewin' on it.

boogie---to hurry

We need to boogie or we're gonna be late!

boogie man---fictitious person that children believe is coming to harm them

Momma, can I sleep with you so the boogie man won't get me?

book it---to leave hastily; to do something quickly

We need to book it or we're gonna be late.

book read---educated

I ain't book read, but I've got plenty of common sense.

boonies---"boondocks"; an isolated area away from civilization; any "out of the way" place

I'd probably go see Granny more often if she didn't live out in the boonies.

boss man---the boss; an employer; a supervisor

I don't know if I can get off for the fishin' trip. I guess it depends what kinda mood the boss man is in.

bottom---a low lying area of land, usually marshy

I got the four-wheeler stuck down in the bottom. I need someone to come help pull me out.

bottom of the barrel--- of the worst quality

The only reason you got that car for so cheap is because it was the bottom of the barrel.

boudin---a spicy Cajun sausage made with rice and meat; pronounced "BOOdan"

Try a piece of this shrimp boudin that Merle cooked.

bought the farm---died

It's been years since Granny bought the farm, but I still miss her.

bouncin' off the walls--- extremely hyper, over active, nervous

My little sister is constantly bouncin' off the walls.

bound to---certain to

With all those clouds in the sky, it's bound to start raining.

Bourbon Street---a street in the French Quarter of New Orleans infamous for it's wild nightlife.

As long as I live, I will never forget seein' my sister pukin' on Bourbon Street. That was one wild night!

'bout---about, almost, nearly

I 'bout had a heart attack when I saw the bill!

box one's ears---to punish, assault

You best clean your room or your Daddy's gonna box your ears when he gets home!

boy howdy---a general exclamation used to emphasize it's context

Boy howdy! That's some damn hot chili!

boy, I mean--- (see "I mean to tell you")

Dixie Jean: *Damn it's hot!*
Lucy Lou: *Boy, I mean!*

britches---pants or underpants

Honey, would you put your britches on and go to the store for me?

bro/bra---brother, friend

What's up, Bra? Long time, no see.

brown sugar---reference to the libido of black women

Uncle Willie came back from N'Orluns talkin' about bourbon and brown sugar.

brung---brought

I brung 15 pounds of potato salad to the picnic and not a single person ate any.

Bubba---a "good ol' boy"; a redneck or hick; usually implies a slow mentality

Sara: *So what's your brother like?*
Beth: *You wouldn't like him. He's a Bubba.*

bug---an illness

Everyone at the office is out sick. Must be a bug goin' around.

buggy---a shopping cart

Go fetch me a buggy so we don't have to carry everything.

built like a brick shithouse---of high quality, very attractive; said of a beautiful woman

You should see Bill's sister. She's built like a brick shithouse!

bull corn---expression of disbelief

Oh bull corn! You can't sit here and tell me a lie like that. I know better.

bull hockey---expression of disbelief

Bull hockey! I know you only called to borrow money.

bullshit---1) expression of disbelief

Wilbur: *I shot a twelve point buck yesterday!* Cooter: *Bullshit! You couldn't shoot the broad side of a barn!*

2) unacceptable

My boss didn't give us a Christmas bonus this year and frankly, I think that's bullshit!

3) to mislead, manipulate

DJ: *Caller #10, you are the thousand dollar grand prize winner!* Winner: *No way! Are you bullshittin' me?*

4) to talk about nothing in particular

I just called to bullshit with you.

bush hoggin'

bush hoggin'---driving off-road for fun

Hey Skeeter, let's get liquored up and go bush hoggin' tonight. Ya wanna?

bushwhacked---ambushed

The troop was marching home when they were bushwhacked from the North.

butt-ass necked--- completely naked

She come a runnin' into the livin' room, butt-ass necked!

butter beans---lima beans

When I was a kid, I couldn't stand the taste of butter beans.

buttercup---a term of endearment

C'mere, buttercup, and hug your Granny's neck.

by---1) short for "bayou" (see "bayou")

I long for the days of fishin' on the by.

2) at

You can sleep by my house tonight if ya want to.

~C~

cain't---pronunciation of "can't"

I got my pickup stuck in the mud and I cain't get it out.

Cajun---a resident or native of Southern Louisiana; descendant of French immigrants; pertaining to Cajun culture

Them Cajuns sho' know how to throw a party!

can't beat that with a stick---"that can't be beat"; "You can't complain about good fortune"

Joe Bob: *My boss closed the shop down for a week. I'm goin' to Disneyworld.* Bobby Joe: *Well, you can't beat that with a stick.*

can't carry a tune in a bucket---said of someone who sings poorly

Poor girl. She's pretty to look at, but she can't carry a tune in a bucket.

can't hardly---"can hardly"; a common double negation

I'm so excited I can't hardly set still!

can't see straight---to be impaired; adds emphasis to the cause

I'm so damn tired I can't see straight!

carry---to drive

Could someone please carry me to the store?

carryin' on---making excess noise, creating commotion, celebrating

What's all that carryin' on up there? You kids best get to sleep!

catawampus---crooked, out of place, misaligned

Will you straighten that picture while you're up. It's all catawampus.

catty-corner---diagonal to/from

In checkers, you can only move catty-corner from the square you're on.

caught with one's pants down---caught off guard or unprepared; caught committing a mischievous deed

Iris: *I heard you caught ol' Jethro with his pants down.* Daisy: *Yeah, he told me he was workin' late, but I saw his car down at the strip club.*

chaps my ass/hide---makes me mad

Willie took my fishin' pole without askin'. That really chaps my ass!

chaw---chewing tobacco

Grandma used to keep her chaw in her apron pocket.

chew(ing) the fat---to talk, talking

My wife sits on the phone chewin' the fat all day.

chicken fried steak---tenderized beef dipped in an egg, milk, and flour mixture and fried in oil

Chicken fried steak is a standard dish at any Southern restaurant.

Chicken Ranch---a once infamous Texas brothel

I've heard many a tale about the Chicken Ranch out near La Grange.

chickenscratch---1) poor handwriting

I can't read this chickenscratch.

2) an insignificant amount (of money)

I'm tired of workin' my fingers to the bone for chickenscratch.

chickenshit---a coward, cowardly

Don't be such a chickenshit. There's no reason to be afraid of the dark.

chigger---a parasitic flea found in forests

I think I got into some chiggers in the woods. My ankles itch.

chilluns---"children"

Gather up the chilluns and let's go get some ice cream.

chitlins---"chitterlings"; fried pig intestines

We're havin' chitlins for dinner. Mmmmm.

chompin' at the bit--- overly anxious

Joe's lookin' forward to the baseball game. He's just chompin' at the bit to play.

Chooseday---common pronunciation of "Tuesday"

I'm off next Chooseday. Let's go fishin'.

chunk---to throw

We spent the whole day chunkin' rocks in the lake.

chunkin' rock---a rock of the proper size and shape to make a worthy projectile

I don't see any more good chunkin' rocks. I think we done throwed 'em all.

chunk of change---a large quantity of money

I lost a pretty good chunk of change at the casino.

cipher---to do arithmetic, to count

I never did learn to cipher much. I still have to take my shoes off to count to 20.

city folk---people accustomed to life in the city; urbanites

You city folk wouldn't know what to do without your cell-phones and pizza delivery.

clean one's plow---to punish, to assault

I'm gonna clean your plow if you don't go mow the yard!

clobber---to assault

I used to clobber my sister daily when we were kids.

clod-hoppers---boots, shoes

Get your clod-hoppers off my coffee table.

cobbler---a fruit pie with a thick upper crust

I'd drive a thousand miles for some of Momma's peach cobbler.

coke---any carbonated beverage; a soda pop

What kind of coke do you want?

cold as a well digger's ass---very cold

Ma: *Go out and get us some more firewood.*
Pa: *Shit no! It's cold as a well digger's ass out there!*

cold as a witch's tit---very cold

I think he's dead. He's as cold as a witch's tit.

cold drink---a carbonated beverage; a soda pop

Come on in outta the heat and have yourself a cold drink.

colored---African-American; may be considered offensive

Once upon a time, white folks and colored folks couldn't eat at the same restaurant together.

colt---a pronunciation of "cold"

Southern winters ain't very colt.

come---1) came

The Sun come up about an hour ago.

2) upon the occurrence of

Come Sun up, we're goin' fishin'.

Come again---a request for one to repeat oneself

Come again. I didn't hear you.

come back---a rebuttal, usually in response to an insult

Willie insulted me and, for the life of me, I just couldn't think of a good come back.

come back to bite me on the ass---"got me in the end"; when bad karma comes around full circle

All that tax evasion came back to bite me on the ass.

come hell or high water---one way or another, no matter what

I'm gonna retire by forty come hell or high water!

come see---come here, come look

Mildred, come see! I need to talk to you.

come unglued---to become enraged

I come unglued when I heard Kennedy was shot.

come uppins---deserved punishment; a scolding

Little Bessie got her come uppins for talkin' out loud in church.

comme ci, comme ca---(French) "like this, like that"; equivalent to "so-so"; neither good nor bad; pronounced "CUMsee, CUMsah"

Amy: *How'd you like the movie?*
Courtney: *Eh, comme ci, comme ca.*

Como?---pronunciation of "Comment?" (French); How?; What?

Maw: *Are you listenin' to me?*
Damon: *Como?*
Maw: *I didn't think so.*

conniption (fit)---a tantrum, an outburst of anger

Yes, you can have some ice cream. Don't have a conniption fit.

cook off---an organized, festive, cooking contest

We won third place in the annual chili cook off.

cook out---gathering where food is prepared outdoors

We're havin' a cook out down at the park this weekend.

cook up---to prepare food

Pick up some potatoes on your way home. I'm gonna cook us up a stew.

'coon---1) a derogatory reference to an African-American

(The use of this term is often considered offensive.)

2) a raccoon

We've got a bad problem with 'coons gettin' in the trash.

'coon ass---a person born, raised, or living in Louisiana, particularly the Northern portion

Most of my relatives are coon ass.

cooter---1) a turtle

I accidently run over a cooter crossin' the road this mornin'.

2) a vagina

That woman's jeans was so tight, you could see her cooter just as plain as day!

cop a squat---a command to squat or sit down

Cop a squat and take a look at this here spider.

corn bread---bread made from cornmeal, eggs, and milk

MaMa used to make corn bread every Saturday for breakfast.

corn cracker---a poor white farmer/person; may be considered offensive

His whole family is nothin' but a bunch of no good corn crackers!

corner store---any convenience store, not necessarily on a corner

Go on down to the corner store and pick me up some lottery tickets and a pack of smokes.

corn fed---of healthy stature or high quality

There's plenty of good, corn fed women in the South.

corn pone---corn bread made without milk or eggs (see "corn bread")

When I was a kid, we were so poor, we could barely afford corn pone.

corn squeezin's---corn liquor, moonshine (see "moonshine")

Grandpa keeps his corn squeezin's locked up in the liquor cabinet.

cotton pickin'---lousy, of poor quality

That cotton pickin' son of a bitch stole my woman.

Cotton State---a nickname for Alabama

The Cotton State has very little Gulf Coast shoreline.

couillon---(French) a moron, idiot, dumbass; pronounced "COOyone"

Russell: *I think I stepped in cow shit.*
Monique: *Couillon!*

couldn't carry a tune in a bucket---said of someone with absolutely no singing ability

The dogs start howlin' when Ellie starts singin'. She couldn't carry a tune in a bucket.

couldn't hit the broad side of a barn---an insult to someone who's a bad shot or a bad throw; one with bad aim

What makes you think the coach is gonna let you be the quarterback? You couldn't hit the broad side of a barn with a beach ball.

count one's blessings---to be thankful for something

I count my blessin's every day that I wasn't born a Yankee!

country bumpkin---a rural bred person, someone accustomed to life in the country

There's somethin' to be said for country bumpkins. They're not stressed out like us city folk.

country mile---a moderate distance

I haven't seen a house in a country mile.

cousin---any male to whom you are referring; not necessarily one's own cousin

Hey there, cousin. Could you give me directions to Birmingham?

cow chip---cow dung

This is open range, so watch out for cow chips.

cow chip throwing contest---a contest in which contestants throw cow dung for distance

I won $100 in the cow chip throwin' contest last Saturday.

cow kiss---a very wet kiss; to lick another's face

I hate goin' to grandma's. She always gives me cow kisses.

cow lick---a tuft of hair that sticks up

The other kids at school pick on Jr. about his cowlick.

cow patty/pie---cow dung

I smell something. Did you step in a cow patty?

cow poke---a cowboy, country person, redneck or the like

Them cow pokes out there at that dude ranch were some mighty hospitable people.

cow sense---common sense, good judgement

She's a nice gal, but she ain't got a lick of cow sense.

cow tippin'---a prank involving the "pushing over" of an unsuspecting cow.

Hey, y'all want to go cow tippin' tonight?

cow town---a town that generates most of it's income from cattle ranching

Amarillo has always been a cow town.

cracker---a derogatory reference to a Caucasian person; a poor white Southern farmer

(The use of this term is often considered offensive.)

cracklin' bread---corn bread made with ground pork skins (see "corn bread")

Momma used to make cracklin' bread for special occasions.

crackin' a gut---laughing

I got detention for crackin' a gut in class today.

crack the window---to open the window partially

Hey man, crack that window. It's hot in here.

crawdad/ crawdaddy--- (see "crawfish")

Otis is down at the bayou fishin' fer crawdads.

crawfish---1) a crayfish; a crustacean popularly eaten in the South

Crawfish are on sale down country market. Let's go get some and have a boil.

2) to break a promise, to change one's mind

You said I could borrow your car last week. You're not crawfishin' are ya?

crawfish boil---a get together where crawfish is boiled and eaten (see "crawfish")

You goin' to the crawfish boil down at the beach this weekend?

Creole---a combination of Southern French and Black cultures

There's nothing quite like Creole cookin'.

crick---1) a creek

Me and sis are goin' fishin' down at the crick.

2) a sharp pain or stiffness

I've had a crick in my neck all week.

critter---an animal or insect

Critters came into our campground and ate all our food.

crocodile tears---tears conjured for a deceitful purpose, "false" tears

Momma, I swear I didn't hit her. Those are crocodile tears.

crooked as a rattler in a cactus patch---dishonest; deceitful

I wouldn't trust him if I were you. He's as crooked as a rattler in a cactus patch.

cue---short for "barbecue" (see "bar-B-Q")

I'm havin' a cue this weekend. Y'all come on over.

cup towel---a dish towel

Grab that cup towel and make yourself useful.

cuss---1) a difficult or annoying person

Don't you talk back to me, you little cuss!

2) to curse

I won't stand for no cussin' in my house!

cut---to turn something on or off

Cut the light off, will ya? I'm trying to sleep.

cut a rug---to dance

C'mon, baby. Let's go down to the ice house and cut a rug.

cut the tail off the dog---"get to the point"; to make a long story short

Cut the tail off the dog already. Can't you see I'm in a hurry?

cutie pie---1) term of endearment

Hey cutie pie! What's your name?

2) a pretty girl

How did someone as ugly as you end up with a cutie pie like her?

cut out---to leave

I'm gonna cut out early today, if you don't mind.

cut the light on---turn the light on

Cut the light on. You'll ruin your eyes tryin' to read in the dark.

cuttin' up---talking or laughing

I got kicked out of school for cuttin' up in class.

cuz'---short for "cousin" (see "cousin")

Hey cuz'! What have you been up to?

~D~

Daddy---father; commonly used by Southern adults as well as children

Daddy called and asked me to come mow his yard.

Dadgummit---a mild expletive expressing contempt or annoyance

Dadgummit! I forgot to get milk while I was at the store.

Dagnabbit--- (see "Dadgummit")

Dagnabbit, dog! Quit shittin' on my floor.

Daisy Dukes---very short cut-off jeans; refers to Daisy Duke's shorts in the tv show "The Dukes of Hazzard"

That gal draws plenty of attention when she wears her Daisy Dukes.

damnedest---1) best effort

I can't dance, but I'll try my damnedest.

2) strangest, most bewildering

I once caught a fish that looked like Elvis. It was the damnedest thing ya ever did see!

damn near---almost

I got bit by a snake once and it damn near killed me.

damn straight--- positively, absolutely

Damn straight, I shot him! That's what he gets for breakin' into my house.

damn Yankee---
   (see "Yankee")

This country would be a much better place if we could just get rid of all the damn Yankees!

dang---euphemism for
   "damn"

Dang it! I just can't seem to peel a tater without cuttin' myself.

Darlin'---1) "Darling";
   a term of endearment;

Well, hello Darlin'! What brings you by?

   2) adorable, cute, or
   endearing

I saw the most darlin' little sun dress at the mall today!

darn tootin'---positively,
   absolutely, assuredly
   (see "damn straight")

Jimmy: *Boy, it sure is hot.*
Brenda: *Darn tootin'!*

dat---a common
   pronunciation of "that"

Whar'd you get dat fancy new car?

dawg---a common
   pronunciation of "dog"

My dawg's expectin' pups any day now.

dawggonnit---mild
   expletive expressing
   contempt or annoyance

Dawggonnit! My favorite show's about to come on and the cable went out.

day-ed---pronunciation
   of "dead"

Someone shot Leroy in his hay-ed. Now he's day-ed.

Decoration day---
   Memorial day

Most people don't have to work on Decoration day.

deef---pronunciation of "deaf"

You'll have to speak up. I'm deef in one ear and cain't hear out t'other.

deer lease/deerwoods---land leased for hunting

We're goin' camping at the deerwoods this weekend.

Delta blues---a style of blues music as opposed to "Chicago" blues, for example. Refers to the Mississippi River Delta

Robert Johnson is known as "King of the Delta Blues".

dern---euphemism for "damn"

These dern mosquitoes are about to drive me plumb crazy.

dern near---almost

I fell asleep drivin' and dern near wrecked my car.

Devil is beatin' his wife---said to be the cause of rain on a sunny day

I can't believe it's rainin' on such a beautiful day! The Devil must be beatin' his wife!

diddly (squat)---nothing

The boys came back from huntin' this mornin'. They didn't get diddly-squat.

differ'nt animal---a strange or unrelated object or situation

I know a lot about history, but quantum physics is a whole differ'nt animal.

dirt dauber---a wasp that builds its home by forming mud into tubes and chambers

I was climbin' around in the barn and got stung by a dirt dauber.

dis---a common pronunciation of "this"

I do believe dis is the best peach cobbler I've ever had.

ditty---a short, basic song

Pick up that guitar and play me a little ditty.

Dixie---the South

My Grandpa is comin' to visit. He's never been to Dixie.

Dixie cup---a small, disposable, paper cup

Mom, can I have some Dixie cups for my lemonade stand?

Dixieland---(see "Dixie")

I may travel the world, but Dixieland will always be home.

doesn't hold water--- (see "doesn't wash")

You're four hours late! The "busload of drowning babies" excuse doesn't hold water.

doesn't wash--- doesn't work; doesn't withstand scrutiny

Her story doesn't wash. I think she did it!

dogs---feet

I've been on my dogs all day. I need to sit down for a while.

---

dolled up---well dressed, well groomed

Missy spent $100 gettin' dolled up for the dance.

done---already

I done ate supper, but I'm still hungry.

done did---already did

Chuck: *Throw another log on the fire.*
Russell: *I done did!*

Don't count your chickens before they're hatched.---"Don't act prematurely."; "Don't rely on something yet unknown."

He hasn't accepted your offer yet. Don't count your chickens before they're hatched.

Don't get your feathers ruffled.---"Don't get upset or angry."

Now don't get your feathers ruffled. He wasn't insulting you. You just took it wrong.

Don't let the door hit you in the ass.---an insulting command for one to leave immediately

Ex-wife: *Fine! I'm leaving!*
Ex-husband: *Good! Don't let the door hit you in the ass!*

Don't look a gift horse in the mouth.---"Don't look for fault in good fortune"

Buddy: *I only got a 50 cent raise this year.*
Jimmy: *Well, don't look a gift horse in the mouth. That's 50 cents more than you were makin'.*

---

don't make me no nevermind---"doesn't matter to me"

Ma: *Do you want peas or carrots with supper?*
Pa: *It don't make me no nevermind. Whatever you want.*

Don't piss on my back and tell me it's rainin'.---"Don't lie to me." "Don't play me for a fool."

You want me to believe it's snowin' in Miami? Don't piss on my back and tell me it's rainin'.

Don't put all your eggs in one basket.---"Leave yourself open to other possibilities."; "Don't risk everything together."

If you're gonna play the stock market, be sure not to put all your eggs in one basket.

Don't that beat all?---"Isn't that outrageous?"

I can't believe he ate the whole pie! Don't that just beat all?!

doodle bug---a pill bug; a tiny insect with a segmented shell that can roll up into a ball in defense

When I was a kid, I used to catch doodle bugs in Granny's back yard.

dooger---a name for an object used in lieu of it's proper label

Hand me that dooger by your foot.

doohickey---(see "dooger")

What do ya call that doohickey for opening wine bottles?

dope---a Coca-Cola or other carbonated beverage

Will you fetch me a dope while you're up?

double dog dare---a final, insulting challenge to someone to do something

I double dog dare you to to eat a tadpole!

Do what?---"What did you say?"; an expression of disbelief

Ma: *I won the lottery this mornin'!*
Pa: *Do what?*

down home---reminiscent of home or family

It's been a long time since I've had real down home cookin'.

down in the mouth--- depressed, upset

You look down in the mouth. What's wrong?

down in the skillet---in the Texas panhandle

I've got relatives down in the skillet.

downright---absolutely, very

The weather is downright nasty today.

down to a gnat's ass--- precisely, accurately

I got that ol' Chevy tuned right down to a gnat's ass.

draw---a dry creek

There's some sand dunes on the other side of the draw.

drawers---pants or underpants

I went to the beach today and I've still got sand in my drawers.

drawl---term used to describe the slow Southern manner of speech; the Southern accent

City folk tend to have less of a drawl than the country folk.

dressin' gown---a night gown

Granny doesn't do much anymore. She just sits around in her dressin' gown eatin' beef jerky.

drizzle---light, misty rain

The weather man said it might drizzle, but there won't be a storm.

drug---dragged

I drug that deer about a half a mile before I realized it weren't dead.

drunker than Cooter Brown---heavily intoxicated

Wilbur: *Man, I tell you what, I was drunker than Cooter Brown last night!* Bubba: *Yeah, so I've heard.*

druthers---one's desires, wishes, wants

If I had my druthers, we'd be goin' to Disney World this summer.

dry spell---a period of time void of rain

My crops are gonna die if there don't come an end to this here dry spell.

duck fit---a crazed expression of anger; a temper tantrum

Mom threw a duck fit when I told her I scratched her car.

duds---clothes, attire

Whar'd you get those spiffy duds?

duke---a clenched fist

Alright, you done pissed me off. Put up your dukes.

duke it out---to fight with one's fists

I'm tired of listenin' to y'all argue. Why don't y'all just duke it out?

dumplin's---balls of dough boiled in a thick stew, or filled with fruit or meat, i.e. chicken dumplin's, squirrel dumplin's, apple dumplin's

Grandma always makes squirrel dumplin's when we come to visit.

durn---euphemism for "damn"

These durn mosquitoes are drivin' me nuts!

dust devil---a whirlwind full of dust

I got caught in a dust devil out in the parkin' lot.

~E~

eatin' high on the hog---successful; prosperous

I've been eatin' high on the hog ever since I got this new job.

eatin's---food

Crawfish and bar-B-Q is what I call good eatin's.

eat up---command for one to eat

Y'all eat up now. There's plenty of food for everybody to have a second helpin'.

egg on---to incite; to instigate; to pressure someone to do something

No matter how much your brothers egg you on, you shouldn't do the stupid things they tell you to do.

enough to choke a horse---a large quantity

That woman wears enough makeup to choke a horse.

enough to make a preacher lay his bible down---enough to incite anyone to violence

Poor Willie caught his ol' lady in bed with his best friend. That's enough to make a preacher lay his bible down.

enough to wear the horns off a billy goat---enough to irritate or annoy excessively

Damn, kid, you talk enough to wear the horns off a billy goat!

-est---suffix often used improperly to add extra emphasis

That is the talkinest woman I've ever met. She just never shuts up!

et---eaten, ate

Vern: *Have you et yet?*
Bubba: *Yep, I et too much.*

étouffeè---a Cajun stew of shellfish or chicken served over rice

There's this restaurant on Bourbon street that has the absolute best étouffeè.

evenin'---"evening"; often used instead of "afternoon"

I cain't go nowhere 'til Pa gets home and he don't get off work 'til 2 o'clock this evenin'.

ever'---every

Ever' time I go to the beach I get stung by a jellyfish.

ever did see---have ever seen

She was the purtiest woman I ever did see.

ever'where's---"everywhere"

I don't know where it could be. I looked ever'where's.

everwhichway/ everywhichaways---in every direction

She threw a handful of firecrackers in the fire and people went runnin' everywhichaways.

~F~

fair to middling---average; mediocre

Travis: *Hey Liz. How are you doin'?*
Elizabeth: *Fair to middlin', I reckon.*

falling out---a dispute or argument resulting in the termination of a relationship

We had a fallin' out about three years back and I ain't spoke to her since.

fancy---1) to prefer, desire

I kinda fancy a steak for supper.

2) to have amorous feelings for

Maybe you should call her. I think she kinda fancies you.

3) of exceptional quality

Aunt Bernice is comin' for dinner. We'd better break out the fancy silverware.

far---a common pronunciation of "fire"

My house caught on far and I lost everything I owned.

fast time---daylight savings time

Man, I just can't seem to get used to this fast time.

fat back---salt pork

You hungry? I've got some fat back left over from the Bar-B-Q.

fat, dumb, and happy--- blissfully unaware; ignorant

Aunt Mildred was always too fat, dumb, and happy to catch the young'uns in the cookie jar.

faubourg---(Cajun) a suburb, neighborhood

There ain't no crime in my faubourg.

favor---to resemble

I think I look like my Dad, but most people tell me I favor my mother.

fed up---disgruntled to an extreme degree

It's only April and I'm already fed up with the heat this year.

feisty---playful, hyper, ornery

The cat sure is feisty today. Did somebody give her some catnip?

feller---fellow; a male person

Defendant: *I swear I've never seen that feller before in my life!*

fell outta the ugly tree (and hit every branch on the way down)--- denotes that person being spoken of is extremely physically unattractive

She's a wonderful girl, but she has a hard time gettin' a date on account of she fell outta the ugly tree and hit every branch on the way down.

fer---for

What'd ya go an' do that fer?

fer/fur piece---
a moderate distance

Bubba: *You wanna walk down to the creek?*
Cletus: *The creek's a fer piece up the road. Let's take the four-wheelers.*

fess up---confess,
tell the truth

I think Leroy did it, but he'd never fess up in a million years.

fetch---to retrieve;
command to retrieve

Can you fetch me a soda while you're up?

fetchin'---attractive;
beautiful

Well, hello Missy. You look quite fetchin' tonight.

fib---a lie

You're not tellin' me a fib, are you?

fiddle---a violin

Man, that feller could play the fiddle like it was nobody's business.

fiddle fart---to procrastinate
or waste time

Quit fiddle fartin' around. We're gonna be late!

fiddlesticks---1) a mild
expletive expressing
frustration

Oh fiddlesticks! I left my grocery list at the house.

2) a mild expletive
expressing disbelief

Bonnie: *I won the lottery.*
Clyde: *Oh fiddlesticks! You did not!*

fidget---to move nervously
or sporadically; to
manipulate unnecessarily

How am I supposed to cut your hair if you won't quit fidgetin'?

figger---pronunciation of "figure"; to calculate, to understand

The way I figger it, you owe me five hundred dollars!

fightin' words---statement(s) that could incite someone to violence

Jethro: *Your woman's lookin' pretty good.*
Cletus: *Watch it! Them's fightin' words!*

filé---powdered sassafras leaves; used to thicken gumbo

Boudreaux, run down to the store and get me some more filé.

fine and dandy---1) in a perfect state; well and good

Bessie Mae: *How's your wife and kids?*
Billy Bob: *They're just as fine and dandy as they can be!*

2) irrelevant; beside the point

Son: *Can I go fishin'?*
Pa: *No. You're grounded.*
Son: *But I finished my homework.*
Pa: *Well that's fine and dandy, but you're still grounded.*

finnin' to---(see "fixin' to")

I'm finnin' to go to the store. Do you need anything?

fire up---to start, to turn on

Go out and fire up the four-wheeler. We need to go haul some wood.

fired up---1) excited

The concert's tonight. I'm fired up and ready to go.

2) angry

Don't go near mom. She's all fired up about somethin'.

fish fry---a gathering where fish is cooked and eaten

Gus is havin' a fish fry this weekend at his house.

fishin' pole---a fishing rod; a rod and reel

Go grab your fishin' pole and meet me down at the river.

fisticuffs---a fight; fighting for sport

The argument between Willie and Joe went on for days and, in the end, came down to fisticuffs.

fittin'---appropriate

It ain't fittin' fer a lady to sit spread-eagle.

fit to be tied---very angry or upset

Bubba lost his job last Friday and he's still fit to be tied.

fixed---spayed or neutered in reference to cats and dogs

I have to get my dog fixed next weekend.

fixin's---condiments; the various ingredients of a meal

Looks like we've got all the fixin's for a damn fine Bar-B-Q.

fixin' to---the state of almost being ready; planning to; about to

Mom: *Go clean your room!*
Son: *I'm fixin' to.*

fix one's red wagon---to punish or get even

Poachin' on my land, is he? I'll fix his red wagon.

flat out---absolutely; without reason; adds emphasis to what is being stated

I'm sorry I missed your birthday. I just flat out forgot.

flustered---frustrated, upset

When Mary lost the beauty pageant, she got so flustered she cried.

fly off the handle---to become angry or enraged

Momma flew off the handle when she caught me colorin' on the wall.

folks---1) parents

I can't go out tonight. My folks are comin' to town.

2) people

How are you folks doin' this evenin'?

follow---to understand

I'll meet you in front of the airport at 9:30. You follow me?

for certain/for sure---certainly, surely

I'm gonna fail economics for sure.

for to---in order to

I have to get up early for to make it to work on time.

for true---surely, definitely, really

Do you really love me for true?

four-lane---a highway

Better yet, I'll meet you at the corner of Airport Boulevard and the four-lane.

French Quarter---the most famous area of New Orleans, known for it's history, architecture, music, and nightlife

You'd have to be dead to not have a good time in the French Quarter.

fret---to worry

Don't fret Momma. I'll be careful crossin' the road.

Friday week---one week from the next Friday (used with any day of the week)

I have a meeting with the President Friday week.

fritter---batter fried fruit or meat

Every Sunday, Dad goes to the donut shop to get apple fritters.

frog sticker---a pocket knife

Grandpa can sit on the porch for hours, whittlin' away with his frog sticker.

from the getgo---from the beginning

That presentation was doomed from the getgo.

full of piss and vinegar---exhibiting youthful exuberance and vigor

When I was young, and full of piss and vinegar, I wasn't afraid of nothin'.

full up---full

I'm all full up on pecan pie. I couldn't eat another bite.

funnin'---joking

Don't take it personally. I was only funnin'.

funny-haha---humorous, comical; used in conjunction with "funny peculiar"

Do you mean funny-haha or funny-peculiar?

funny-peculiar---strange or homosexual

I mean he's funny-peculiar. That boy's as queer as a three dollar bill.

further---farther

I walked further today than I ever have in my life.

fuss---1) to complain

What are you fussin' about?

2) to scold

Mom's been fussin' at me all mornin'.

fuss and feathers---said of someone making a big deal of nothing

Don't pay him no mind. He's all fuss and feathers.

fuss bucket---a cranky or complaining person, usually a child

Well aren't you just a little fuss bucket! Maybe you need a nap.

~G~

gal---girl

The prettiest gal I've ever met was a Texan.

galley---porch

I enjoy my Sundays sittin' on the galley drinkin' lemonade.

galley nipper---a mosquito

I'm goin' inside. These damn galley nippers are drivin' me nuts!

gallivantin'---wandering around

Betty: *Have you seen Bubba lately?*
Alice: *He's probably just off gallivantin' around somewhere. He'll turn up.*

galoot---a fool

I wonder if that galoot knows he's about to walk into traffic.

gander---to look

Take a gander at the size of that watermelon.

gator---an alligator

I found a gator in my backyard once when I lived in Florida.

geed when one should have hawed---"gee" and "haw" are verbal commands for a horse or mule to turn right or left respectively. This is said of someone who did the opposite of what he/she should have done, to a negative effect

I told him not to gamble his last dollar away, but he didn't listen. He went ahead and geed when he should have hawed.

geetar---a common pronunciation of "guitar"

Why don't you pick up that geetar and play me a tune.

genteel---refined, well mannered

Rarely do I meet a man as genteel as yourself.

Georgia credit card---a short length of hose used to siphon gasoline out of a vehicle

I don't have a gas can, but I keeps a Georgia credit card in the back of my pickup.

Georgia ice cream---grits

I can make a meal out of Georgia ice cream alone.

get/git---command for someone or something to go away

Git! Stay out of my flowerbed! Damn it, I said git!

get after it---command to hurry; to commence doing something

Boy, I told you to mow the yard. Now get after it!

get a move on--- (see "get after it")

Get up and get ready for school. Get a move on!

get back to one's rat killin'---to resume what one was previously doing

Well, that's enough chit chat. I need to get back to my rat killin'.

get glad in the same pants one got mad in---to get over that which made one angry; used sarcastically to mean "tough, that's the way it is"

She's mad at me for not callin' last night, but she can just get glad in the same pants she got mad in.

get gone---to leave

Hurry up! We gotta get gone already.

Getonattaheaw!/ Gitownaddahair!--- pronunciations of "Get on out of here!"; command for an animal, usually a dog, to go away

I thought I told you to git! Now gitownaddahair!

get one's duck's in a row---to prepare; to plan ahead

You better get all your ducks in a row before you retire.

get one's ears lowered--- to get a haircut

Ma took me down to the barber shop to get my ears lowered.

get the hell out of dodge--- to leave in a hurry

If we don't get the hell out of dodge, we'll never make it by morning.

gettin' into it---fighting, arguing

I didn't get a wink of sleep. The couple upstairs were gettin' into it all night.

get together---a social gathering

We're havin' a get together at my house next weekend.

get up---clothes, uniform, outfit, costume

You look mighty silly in that get up!

giddyup---command for a horse to move forward

Damn horse! When I say "giddyup", I mean GIDDYUP!

gig---a wooden pole with a sharp spike or hook on one end used to catch frogs or fish

Go fetch a couple of gigs and meet me down by the pond.

giggin'---the act of hunting frogs or fish with a gig (see "gig")

I hope you like frog legs 'cause I'm goin' giggin' tonight.

gimme a holler---"call me", "keep in touch"

Gimme a holler when you get to town.

gist---the premise, the central theme

Yeah, I get the gist, and I'm still not interested.

gitfiddle---a guitar

I once played a gitfiddle owned by Stevie Ray Vaughn.

give out---to become exhausted, to give up, to collapse

I gotta sit down. I think My legs are about to give out.

give someone the what for---to punish, to lecture, to attack

Pa's down at city hall givin' 'em the what for again.

God almighty!---a general exclamation

God almighty, it's hot in here!

God-awful---distasteful, bad, of poor quality

That was the most God-awful movie I've ever seen.

God bless (it)---euphemism for "God damn"; mild expletive expressing contempt or annoyance

God bless it! I forgot I had a pie in the oven!

God-fearin'---religious, believing in Christian virtues

Any normal God-fearin' man would never do such a thing.

God's country---any exceptionally beautiful geographic area

The Mississippi river is God's country to a river boat captain.

God willin' and the creek don't rise---if everything goes as planned

I should be able to afford that boat by June, God willin' and the creek don't rise!

goin' ninety to nothin'---exercising haste; doing something with great energy, enthusiasm, or persistence

You kids need to come in and take a nap. You've been goin' ninety to nothin' all morning.

goin' to hell in a hand basket---leading a life of sin; committing a sinful act; usually used in a jovial sense

I may be goin' to hell in a hand basket, but I sure am enjoying myself.

goan---a pronunciation of "going to"

Cryin' about it ain't goan help none.

goangit---1) going to get

Yer goangit sick if you don't come in and put a jacket on.

2) command for one to locate and retrieve something

Martha, goangit me my shootin' iron.

goin' to town---doing something with much enthusiasm or haste; indulging in something wholeheartedly

I came home and caught my dogs goin' to town chewin' up the furniture.

gonna---going to

Hurry up! I'm not gonna wait forever.

go-oan (go on)---command to go away, usually directed towards a pet

Go-oan, dawg! I'll play with you later.

goober digger/grabber--- a poor country person

I done told you I don't want you marryin' no goddamn goober grabber!

goober (pea)---a peanut

Damn woman! How many boxes of them goobers are you gonna eat?

good God almighty!--- (see "God all mighty")

Good God almighty that sho' smells good! Watcha cookin'?

---

good Lord!--- a common general exclamation

Good Lord, Ben! That was the dumbest joke I've ever heard.

goodness gracious (alive)--- a polite exclamation

Goodness gracious alive! It's rainin' cats and dogs!

good ol' boy---a beer drinkin', truck drivin', fly fishin', fist fightin', gun totin', resourceful, helpful, good-natured, Southern male

Any time you're stuck in the mud, you can count on Willie to help pull you out. He's a good ol' boy.

good people---person(s) of exceptional character

James is the kind of guy who'll help you move. He's good people.

go off half cocked---to act hastily without weighing the consequences, especially while angry

Don't go off half cocked! You'll only make it worse.

gopher---an errand boy, someone who performs odd jobs

I hired a gopher for six bucks an hour.

goshdawgit---a mild expletive expressing contempt or annoyance

Goshdawgit! I meant to turn left back there.

goshdernit--- (see "goshdawgit")

Goshdernit! I just can't seem to find my glasses.

---

gospel truth---the absolute truth; absolutely correct

Pa: *That boy's so dumb, he couldn't find his own ass with a mirror and a map!* Ma: *Ain't that the gospel truth!*

go to shit---to deteriorate; to go bad

If you don't start studyin' more, your grades are gonna go to shit!

gotsda/gotsto---pronunciation of "got to", meaning "have or need to"

I gotsda get me one of those ridin' lawnmowers. I just gotsda!

got to---began; commenced

We got to talkin' and plum lost track of time.

graçious---(Spanish) thank you

You've been a great host. Graçious!

granddaddy---grandfather

My granddaddy always brings me candy when he comes to visit.

grand baby---grandchild

She's got four grandbabies in Texas and two more in Louisiana.

Granny---Grandmother

We're havin' Christmas at Granny's house this year.

grassy ass---humorous pronunciation of Spanish "graçious", thank you (see "graçious")

John: *Here, have a drink.* Clint: *Why grassy ass! Don't mind if I do.*

green---inexperienced, naïve

The new guy doesn't know his ass from a hole in the ground. He's as green as they come.

green beans---string beans

Granny used to grow green beans in her back yard.

greens---green vegetables

Momma always used to make me eat my greens.

grinnin' like a possum eatin' persimmons---a toothy grin or smile

You sure are grinnin' like a possum eatin' persimmons. What's so funny?

gris gris---a voodoo spell or an item used to ward off such spells; pronounced "gree gree"

I always keep a gris gris bag under my pillow for good luck.

grit---a redneck

If it comes down to a fight, I want the grits on my side.

grits---ground, boiled corn

Dad loves grits, but I can't stand 'em.

grounds for an ass whippin'---reason for physical punishment (see "ass whippin")

Badmouthin' my mother is definite grounds for an ass whippin'.

growed---grew

I growed up in a little town in Southern Alabama.

growin' like a weed---
growing very fast

You are just a growin' like a weed. I almost didn't recognize you.

grub---food

What a long day! I'm ready for some grub and a shower.

guaran-damn-tee-ya---
guarantee you

I guaran-damn-tee-ya it's gonna rain tomorrow!

gubment---common
pronunciation of
"government"

Damn gubment's always got it's hands in my wallet.

gulch---a narrow canyon
created by rain run-off

Pa! Get the truck. I shot a deer on the other side of the gulch.

Gullah---a Southern dialect
originating with black
slaves from Africa;
a combination of African
and English words

Damn it! You know I can't understand you when you start speakin' that Gullah!

gully---(see "gulch")

I can't cross the gully in my truck. It's too deep.

gully washer---
a heavy rain

That last gully washer flooded our house.

gumbo---thick soup
containing okra, rice,
seafood, and file powder
(ground sassafras leaves)

PaPa used to make the best gumbo.

gumption---ability, gall, sense, nerve, guts

Whar'd you get the gumption to ask for a raise?

gunshot house---a long, straight house with doors on both ends, such as to allow a straight "shot" through the house without interference by any walls

We finally sold that ol' gunshot house on the far end of our property.

gussied up---well dressed, well groomed

What are you all gussied up for? Got a date?

gut---stomach

She punched me in the gut so hard it knocked the wind out of me.

gwine/gwyne--- a pronunciation of "going (to)"

I'm gwine to the corner store for some bread. Do you need anything?

~H~

hacked off---angry

What are you hacked off about?

hair-trigger---a short temper

Be careful around the boss. He's got a hair-trigger today.

half a mind to--- a strong inclination to

I've got half a mind to pack my bags and hit the road.

hankerin'---hunger, desire

I've got a hankerin' fer some crawfish.

hard road---paved road

I wrecked my bike out on the hard road and skinned myself all up.

hard row to hoe---a difficult situation or endeavor

Missy got pregnant at sixteen. You know that's a hard row to hoe.

harp---a harmonica

I tell ya, I've never seen anyone blow a harp quite like that.

harrowing experience--- a frightful event

I got chewed up by a dog when I was young. It was a harrowing experience.

haul ass---to hurry or leave; command for one to hurry or leave

If you don't haul ass you're gonna be late.

hauled off---suddenly commenced to do something

I thought it was over, but then one guy hauled off and hit the other guy in the face.

Have a good one---request that one have a good day

I'll talk to you later. Have a good one!

have at it---to partake of something

Supper is ready. Y'all have at it.

Hawt---"Heart"; a term of endearment

Come here Hawt, and hug your Momma's neck.

hay-ed---pronunciation of "head"

Poor Timmy. He ain't right in the hay-ed.

head honcho---the person in charge

I'd like to speak to the head honcho. I have a complaint.

heap---a large quantity

I am in a heap of trouble.

heared---heard

Shhhhhh. I heared a noise downstairs.

hear tell---to hear talk of

I hear tell the sheriff's a lookin' fer ya.

heebie jeebies---the frights, the chills, the creeps

Scary movies give her the heebie jeebies.

hellacious---extraordinary

Boy, I had one hellacious hangover this morning!

hellfire and damnation--- an expletive expressing contempt or annoyance

What in hellfire and damnation is goin' on?

hellraisin'---(see "raisin' hell" 2nd definition)

I just got paid and my wife's out of town. I'm lookin' forward to a night of hellraisin'.

hemmin' 'n' hawin'---"bowing up" in a confrontation; fighting

You boys knock off that hemmin' 'n' hawin' afore I whup both yer asses!

here shortly---in a little while

We're goin' out to eat, here shortly.

hern---hers

They've got a set of his and hern towels.

hesh/hush up---command for one to be quiet or stop talking

Hesh up! I can't hear the TV!

het up---angry

Ma's all het up 'cause Pa forgot her birthday.

hey---"hello"; a common greeting

Hey, Bubba! How are you doing?

hick---one bred in the country, one accustomed to life in the country; implies ignorance or low social standing

We don't see too many hicks down here in the city.

hidy/haddy---pronunciation of "howdy"; hello (see "howdy")

Hidy, ma'am. Pleasure to meet your acquaintance.

high strung---hyperactive to a fault

She's high strung, but she gets more work done than any of the other employees.

hightail it---to hurry; command for one to hurry

We best high-tail it if we're gonna catch the 9:00 movie.

high time--- untimely, but not too late; about time

Well it's about high time you came home! I was worried sick.

hillbilly---a rural bred Southerner, one accustomed to life in the country; implies slow mentality

I gave my life to this company only to end up takin' orders from the boss' hillbilly nephew.

hiney---one's backside; buttocks

I see your hiney, all bright and shiny. You better hide it before I bite it.

hisself---himself

He's been full of hisself since the day he discovered mirrors.

hissy fit---expression of anger, a temper tantrum

Don't mind her. She has a hissy fit every time she doesn't get her way.

hitch in one's get-a-long--- a hindering ailment

Granny said she can't come. She's got a hitch in her get-a-long.

hit the hay---to go to bed

I'm gonna hit the hay so I can get up early tomorrow.

hit the road---to leave; command for one to leave

We're gonna be late if we don't hit the road now.

hit the trail---(see "hit the road")

You'd better hit the trail before it starts rainin'.

hoe-down---a dance or party

We're havin' a hoe-down at my house next Friday.

hog heaven---a state of euphoria

Granny baked five pies today. I feel like I'm in hog heaven.

hogwash---nonsense

That story sounds like hogwash to me.

hog wild---crazy; out of control; with much enthusiasm

Pa said he was gonna clean the garage, but he went hog wild and cleaned the whole house.

hold your horses--- command for one to wait or calm down

I know you're anxious, but just hold your horses. We'll go in a minute.

holler---1) to yell, shout

Quit hollerin'. I hear you loud and clear.

2) a hollow; a narrow valley

Ol' man Jefferson lives by himself down in the holler.

3) notify, contact

Holler at me when you get done with your chores.

hollerin' like a stuck pig---screaming loudly and erratically

You are such a sissy! That dentist barely touched your tooth and you started hollerin' like a stuck pig.

hominy---(see "grits")

My dad loves hominy but I think it's disgusting.

honest injun---a declaration of honesty or sincerity

I swear I didn't do it. Honest injun!

Honey---a term of endearment usually reserved for a spouse or sometimes children

Hi, Honey. Whatcha got cookin' fer supper?

Honeychild---a term of endearment; used more casually than "Honey"

Ooh, Honeychild, is that not the most gorgeous sunset ya ever did see?

hongry---a common pronunciation of "hungry"

I hope y'all got dinner ready 'cause I shore am hongry!

honky tonk---1) a style of music emphasizing rolling, bluesy piano

My PaPa was a piano player in a honky tonk band.

2) an upbeat nightclub catering to the honky tonk style of music

They played every honky tonk from here to Beaumont.

hoodoo---a voodoo spirit; an embodiment of bad luck

I keep my lucky rabbit's foot by my bed to ward off the hoodoos.

hoofin' it---traveling on foot

I reckon I'll be hoofin' it 'til my pickup gets outta the shop.

hoot---an amusing person, thing, or event

My grandpa's a hoot when he's been drinkin'.

hootenanny---a party; a celebration

Sounds like they're havin' a hootenanny next door.

hooters---breasts

That gal's got the nicest set of hooters I ever did see!

hootin' 'n' hollerin'---yelling; celebrating loudly causing a scene

It's after midnight! Knock off the hootin' 'n' hollerin' before someone calls the police!

hop to it---a command for one to immediately commence doing something

I want you to clean your room, take out the trash, and wash the car. What are you waitin' for? Hop to it.

hornswoggled---cheated, deceived

They made off with my wallet and my whiskey. I've been hornswoggled again!

horny toad---a lizard with pointed "horns" covering it's body

We used to catch horny toads out in front of Grandma's house in the backwoods.

horse of another color---a separate issue, an unrelated matter

Yeah, I'm still mad at Bubba, but that's a horse of another color.

horsepiddle---a humorous pronunciation of "hospital"

I think I'm goin' into labor. Maybe we should mosey on down to the horse piddle.

horse pill---a large pill

The doctor's got me takin' these damn horse pills again.

horseplay---playing rough or recklessly

No horseplay in the shop! Somebody's gonna get hurt.

horse shit---1) a bad situation

This is horse shit! My ex-wife is suin' me!

2) expletive expressing disbelief

Skeeter: *I got me a date with Morgan Fairchild.* Ennis: *Oh, horse shit! You couldn't get a date from a calendar.*

horse's patoot(y)--- euphemism for "horse's ass" or "asshole"

You can be a real horse's patoot when you want to be.

horsin' around---playing wildly or recklessly

Y'all quit horsin' around before you break something.

hoss---1) pronunciation of "horse"

Thunder was the prettiest hoss I ever did see.

2) derogatory reference to a "tough guy" or a clumsy person

Easy hoss. Don't get yer feathers ruffled.

---

hot hot---"hotter than hot"; extremely hot

Boy, it is hot hot outside today!

hot toddy---a hot drink usually made with water, whiskey, and sugar or honey

Boy it's cold outside! This is good hot toddy weather.

house nigger---an old term for a plantation slave who worked in the house as opposed to the field; may be considered offensive

Billy Boy: *Could you get me a soda?*
Bessie Mae: *I ain't your house nigger!*

How 'bout them apples?---"How do you like that?"

Oh yeah? Well you're grounded 'til your next report card. How 'bout them apples?

How come?---"Why?"

Pa: *We can't go fishin' this weekend.*
Son: *How come?*
Pa: *'Cause there's a storm a comin'.*

How do?---"How do you do?", greetings

How do, stranger?

Howdy---common greeting "How do you do?"; "Hello"

Howdy, Ma'am. Nice day, isn't it?

hug my neck---"give me a hug"

I'mone spank your behind if you don't come here and hug my neck!

---

hunker down---command for one to squat or kneel

This looks like a good place to hunt. Now hunker down and be still.

hunnerd---pronunciation of "hundred"

The place you're lookin' for is about a hunnerd miles up the road.

huntin' snipe---searching for something that cannot be found; attempting something futile (see also "snipe huntin'")

I've looked everywhere for my keys. I feel like I'm huntin' snipe.

hurricane party---a party or gathering for the purpose of enduring a hurricane in good company

We're having a hurricane party at my house. Hurry before the streets flood.

hush my mouth--- a general exclamation

Well, hush my mouth! I ain't seen you in years!

hush puppy---a ball of fried corn meal

Would you like French fries or hush puppies with your fish?

hush your mouth--- command for one to cease talking

Hush your mouth before you say somethin' you'll regret.

~I~

ice house---a small bar

You can always find Pa down at Millie's ice-house.

I don't mind if I do--- expression of acceptance

Clarence: *Would you like some ice cold lemonade?* William: *I don't mind if I do.*

iffen---if

Iffen you look real hard, you just might see a shootin' star.

If it was a snake it would have bit you!---expression used when one locates something that was in close proximity throughout the search

Sister: *I can't find my hat.* Brother: *It's on your head. If it was a snake, it would have bit you!*

if you play your cards right---if you do what you're supposed to do; if you do the right thing; if you make wise decisions

If you play your cards right, maybe your boss will give you a good raise.

I hear ya---"I understand"

Bill: *My wife's always naggin' me. I can't get any peace.* Dave: *I hear ya, man. My wife's the same way.*

I'll be a monkey's uncle---polite version of "I'll be damned"

Well, I'll be a monkey's uncle. I can't believe this ol' car started up on the very first try.

I'll be damned---a general expression/exclamation (see "Well, I'll be")

I'll be damned! Look at all the stars in that country sky!

I'll be dog (gone)---polite version of "I'll be damned"

Well I'll be dog! Don't you just look beautiful!

I'll be jiggers---polite version of "I'll be damned"

Well I'll be jiggers! If it isn't ol' Leroy Brown. How have you been?

I mean to tell you---(see "I'm tellin' you")

Willard: *Damn, it's hot!* Bubba: *Boy, I mean to tell ya! I ain't felt heat like this in years.*

I'mone---pronunciation of "I'm going to"

I'mone get up 'bout six and go fishin' out at Millard's pond.

I'm tellin' you---expression of agreement

Brother: *Nothin' beats Momma's cookin'!* Sister: *Oh, I'm tellin' you!*

I, myself---a common redundance

I, myself, prefer beef over pork.

in back of---behind

We buried that dead bird in back of the barn.

in cahoots---in partnership, in league, conspiring

I think my wife's in cahoots with the devil.

in front of God and everybody---within view of others; in public

Look at those two, makin' out in front of God and everybody. How lude!

Injun---pronunciation of "Indian"

You kids go outside to play cowboys and Injuns.

ink pen---writing utensil using ink, a pen

Could you hand me that ink pen over yonder?

iota---a small quantity of something

The Lord didn't give you one iota of good sense, did He?

ire---pronunciation of "hour"

Sucker: *How long will it take to fix my car?*
Mechanic: *'Bout an ire.*

I reckon---"I'll allow it"; I agree; o.k.

Son: *Can I go over to Bubba's house?*
Ma: *Well, I reckon, but be home for supper.*

I's---1) I am

I's goin' to the store. Anybody need anything?

2) I was

I's about five years old when I got kicked by that horse.

iss 'ere---this here

Iss 'ere is the best pie I've ever had in my whole life.

It's not the size of the dog in the fight...

I tell you what---
expression used to add
emphasis to a statement

*I tell you what, I haven't
had this much fun in
years!*

**It's not the size of the dog
in the fight, it's the size
of the fight in the dog!**---
"It is will, not might, that
matters"

Son: *He'll kill me, Pa.
He's twice my size.*
Pa: *Remember, it's not the
size of the dog in the fight,
it's the size of the fight in
the dog!*

~J~

jabberin'---talking incessantly

Will you quit jabberin' at me? I'm tryin' to watch t.v..

jambalaya---a spicy Cajun stew served over rice

No more jambalaya for me. I'm stuffed!

jamboree---a large, lively celebration involving music

We're goin' to the annual bluegrass jamboree next weekend.

jazz---a style of music native to the South, generally said to have been born in New Orleans by black musicians; was once considered "the devil's music"

I spent four years playin' the sax in a jazz band on Bourbon Street.

jerky---dried, cured meat

My dad makes the best jerky this side of the Pecos.

jibber jabber---meaningless "chit chat"

I don't see how them dang women can sit on the phone jibber jabberin' away all day long.

jig---a lively dance

I'm so happy, I could dance a jig.

jigaboo---a derogatory reference to an African-American

(The use of this term is often considered offensive.)

jim dandy---of good
   quality

That's a jim dandy idea you have. Can I get in on it?

jimmy---1) a penis

She accidentally kicked me in my jimmy.

2) to disengage

I locked my keys in the house. Can you jimmy the lock for me?

John Deere letter---a
   Dear John letter; a letter
   for the purpose
   of terminating a
   relationship

I came home from work one day and found a John Deere letter. I haven't seen her since.

Johnny Reb---a nickname
   for a Southerner

Johnny Reb ain't got no place in his heart for no damn Yankee!

joshin'---kidding, joking

Aw, don't get mad. I was only joshin'.

June bug---a small, brown,
   flying beetle flourishing
   in the summertime

Son: *There's a June bug in my room again.*
Dad: *It won't hurt you. Just go to sleep.*

just about enough---more
   than enough; more than
   one can tolerate

I've had just about enough of this hot, muggy weather.

**just because a chicken
   has wings don't mean
   it can fly**---appearances
   can be deceiving

Yeah, she's purty alright, but just because a chicken has wings don't mean it can fly!

just fell off the turnip truck---insinuates that someone is ignorant naïve

He breaks everything he touches. I think he just fell off the turnip truck.

just for shits and grins--- just for the fun or thrill of it

You wanna camp out in the back yard just for shits and grins?

~K~

keel---common pronunciation of "kill"

I'mone keel you iffen you don't stay off my land!

keel over---1) to die

One minute Grandpa was tellin' a story, and the next minute, he just keeled over.

2) to pass out, to fall over

I don't think you need any more beer. You're about to keel over as it is.

keen---pleasing to the eye, of high quality

That's a keen lookin' bike you got there.

keeper---a fish of legal length, worth keeping

I caught a couple of keepers last weekend, but I haven't had any luck so far today.

keep your britches on--- "be patient"

Supper will be ready in a minute. Keep your britches on!

keep your eyes peeled--- keep watch, pay attention

If you keep your eyes peeled, you might see a shootin' star.

Kentucky Derby--- a horse race held in Louisville, Kentucky

Ol' Sugarfoot placed third in last year's Kentucky Derby.

Key lime pie---a lime pie, named after the limes grown in the Florida Keys

What would you like for desert, ice cream or Key lime pie?

kicker bar---a country and western bar or dancehall

Last thing I remember, we were drinkin' at some kicker bar. How I ended up in jail, I do not know.

kilt---a common pronunciation of "killed"

My boy kilt his first deer last weekend.

kin---relative(s); related

I don't get along with most of my kin.

kinfolk---relatives

I've got kinfolk comin' down from Tennessee this weekend.

kissin' cousins---distant blood relatives

I haven't seen my kissin' cousins since we were kids.

Kiss my grits!---
  1) a general exclamation

Well kiss my grits! I ain't seen you in a coon's age.

  2) a euphemism for "Kiss my ass!"

Ma: *Don't stay out all night drinkin', ya hear?*
Pa: *Kiss my grits!*
Ma: *What?*
Pa: *Nothin' dear.*

KKK---(see Ku Klux Klan)

(The use of this term is often considered offensive)

knee-high to a grasshopper---
short, little, young

Last time I seen you, you was only knee-high to a grasshopper.

knee slapper---something very funny; a joke

I haven't heard that joke in years. That's a real knee slapper!

knock it off---"stop what you are doing"

I'mone whup you good if you don't knock it off!

know better---1) to have a better understanding

Damn it, Junior! You know better than to play with fire!

2) to see through mistruth

Don't you lie to me! I know better than that.

3) to have reason for a contrary opinion

She was late for her own birth. I should've known better than to think she'd be here on time.

knows---know

I knows ever'thin' they is to know 'bout bass fishin'.

Knowuttamean?---"Do you understand?"

Mornin' is gonna come early. Knowuttamean? We should probably get some shut-eye.

Ku Klux Klan---
an infamous white supremacist organization

(The use of this term is often considered offensive.)

~L~

ladybird---a ladybug

Look, Momma! There's a ladybird on the window screen!

lagniappe---something extra given to a customer by a merchant

I bought some hamburger meat and the butcher gave me lagniappe for my dog.

Laissez les bons temps rouler!---(French) "Let the good times roll!"; a popular Cajun expression

You should have seen her. She was stumblin' down Bourbon street hollerin' "Laissez les bons temps rouler!"

land o' cotton--- a nickname for the South

Visitin' New York makes me grateful I was born in the land o' cotton.

layed up---confined to a bed due to an illness or injury

I was layed up with the flu for two weeks straight last year.

learn---teach

Will you learn me how to tie a bowline knot?

learned---educated

I ain't learned in such things as music and fine arts.

learnin'---an education

No sir, I ain't never had no learnin'.

learnt---a common pronunciation of "learned"

I learnt a lot in school, but I wouldn't do it again if ya paid me!

leastways---at least

I don't know why they cut the power off. I paid the bill. Leastways, I think I did.

levee---an embankment beside a river or lake to keep lowlands from flooding

If the levee breaks, we're in big trouble!

lessen---unless

You're gonna get a whippin' lessen you go to bed right now!

libary---pronunciation of "library"

I found a Mark Twain book down at the local libary.

lick---1) to beat up

I ain't skeered of him. I can lick him with one punch.

2) to conquer, to overcome

I think we've almost got it licked.

3) a blow, usually with a clenched fist or a belt

Mom: *How'd you get that bruise?*
Boy: *Aw, me and Bubba was just tradin' licks. He won.*

4) a small quantity

Willie ain't got a lick of sense.

lickety split---quickly; with extreme haste; in an instant

I was sittin' in my deer stand when I noticed a snake quilled up under my chair. Needless to say I got the hell out of that stand lickety split!

lightnin' bug---a firefly

I remember when we used to catch lightnin' bugs in the summertime.

like a bat out of hell---with extreme haste

I threw a firecracker in the tent and Willie came flyin' out of there like a bat out of hell!

like a big dawg---expression used to add emphasis to a statement

The doctor gave me some pain killers when I broke my arm, but it still hurt like a big dawg.

like a bull in a china closet--- wildly, roughly, unruly

There's lots of breakable things in this store, so don't act like a bull in a china closet.

like a bump on a log---still, lazy, dazed

She's so depressed. She just sits in front of the t.v. like a bump on a log.

like a chicken with its head cut off---gyrating wildly

I pulled that fish into the boat and it started floppin' around like a chicken with it's head cut off.

like a duck on a June bug---tightly adhered to, closely bonded, relentless

Ol' Blue was on that squirrel like a duck on a June bug.

like a hawk---with intense scrutiny

My parents have watched me like a hawk ever since they caught me sneakin' out my window.

like all get out---with abandon; to an extreme degree

Man, they was fightin' like all get out, but then the law come and took 'em both to jail.

like hammered dog shit---bad, awful, of poor quality, sick

I feel like hammered dogshit! How much did I drink last night?

like stink on shit---tightly adhered to, closely bonded, relentless

When the Sun goes down in Texas, the mosquitoes are on you like stink on shit!

like to---almost

He told me that joke and I like to fell out of my seat.

like two peas in a pod---
1) identical

My sisters are like two peas in a pod. I swear they can read each other's mind.

2) comfortable

Yes dear, I put the children to bed. They're tucked in like two peas in a pod.

line dancin'---popular western style of dance where participants form a line and perform the same series of steps in unison

Boy, I sure did make a fool of myself line dancin' last night!

liquored up---drunk

That boy goes out an' gets liquored up almost ever' night of the week. I don't see how he holds down a job.

lit off/out---left hastily

I don't know where she went. She just got off the phone and lit off down the street.

little bitty---very small

I haven't seen you since you was just a little bitty thang.

little missy---an affectionate nickname for a female

Look here, little missy! I will not tolerate that kind of language in this house.

little old---little, small; insignificant

That's just a little ol' horny toad. He won't hurt you none.

lit up---drunk, intoxicated

Man, I've never seen you this lit up!

lit up like a Christmas tree---extremely intoxicated

She was stumblin' around, lit up like a Christmas tree!

lit up like a firefly---extremely intoxicated

I wasn't the only one lit up like a firefly!

lollygag---to procrastinate; to waste time

Y'all quit lollygaggin' and get back to work!

Lone Star State---a nickname for Texas

Thar's plenty of good deer huntin' down in the Lone Star State.

long about---around; about

It quit rainin' long about 7:30, just after the levy broke.

long hair---a male with long hair; a hippie

We don't take kindly to long hairs in this neck of the woods.

long haul---a long drive; a long time; the whole duration

It's a long haul from Atlanta to Houston.

long johns---thermal underwear

Don't forget to pack your long johns 'cause it's gonna be cold in the Appalachians.

looka/looky here---look here, pay attention

Looky here, Virgil. If you don't start paying attention, you'll never get passed the third grade.

looker---an attractive person

She's not much of a looker but she's got a good heart.

look-see---a look, an inspection

I'm gonna stop at this garage sale and have a look-see.

looks like forty miles of bad road---usually said of someone very ugly or undesirable

I can't stand my mother-in-law. That ol' woman's got a big mouth and she looks like forty miles of bad road!

Loozianna---pronunciation of "Louisiana"

I can't wait to go to Loozianna for Mardi Gras!

Lord almighty!--- (see "God almighty")

Lord almighty! I've never seen so many mosquitoes.

Lord have mercy!--- a general exclamation

Lord have mercy! This rain has just got to end.

Lordy!---a general exclamation

Lordy, lordy! That is one fine lookin' woman!

lose one's britches--- to lose a great deal on a gamble

I lost my britches when the stock market crashed.

lose one's lunch---to vomit

I 'bout lost my lunch when Aunt Bee farted in the car.

Love bug---a small winged insect appearing in swarms during summer and noted for it's ability to fly around while mating

I drove down to Houston this weekend. Now my car's covered in Love bugs.

low down---of poor character

My low down in-laws ain't welcome here.

~M~

ma'am---madam

Excuse me ma'am. Where's the post office?

mad as fire---very angry

Stay away from Helen. It's her time of the month and she's mad as fire.

madder than a wet hen--- extremely angry

I forgot to wash the dishes and Momma got madder than a wet hen.

Magnolia State--- nickname for Mississippi

Aunt Ester moved here from the Magnolia state. She grew up right on the Mississippi river.

make a (big) stink---to bring an issue to light

I wouldn't make a big stink over it. He only shorted you five cents.

make tracks---to leave

It's time to go. Let's make tracks.

makin' groceries--- grocery shopping

Pa: *Where's your Momma?* Son: *She's out makin' groceries.*

MaMa/MawMaw/ MeeMaw---grandmother, great grandmother

I haven't seen MaMa since she moved to the country.

Mardi Gras

Mardi Gras---(French) Fat Tuesday; A festive occasion celebrated around the world just before the beginning of lent, the largest and most widely known American celebration occurring in New Orleans

Everyone should go to Mardi Gras at least once in their lifetime. It's one hell of a good time.

mark my words---"heed what I say"

Mark my words, I will get my revenge.

married off---married

Wilbur married off last year and we ain't seen much of him since.

mash---1) to press

It's a c.b., dear. You have to mash the button to talk.

2) to crush

I'll peel the taters if you'll mash 'em.

Mason-Dixon line---the imaginary boundary between the North and South in terms of culture and philosophy.

The last Yankee that came to town, got his ass kicked all the way back across the Mason-Dixon line.

maverick---a stray, unbranded calf

I caught a maverick wanderin' across my land.

Maw/Mama/Momma---mother

Maw, can I have some ice cream?

Maw and Paw---family owned or non-franchised

That little Maw and Paw restaurant on the corner has the best bar-B-Q in town.

me---1) often used at the end of a statement in Cajun speech

I could not possibly eat one more bite, me. I'm stuffed!

2) myself

I'm gonna buy me a new fishin' pole.

meadow muffin---cow or horse dung

Somethin' stinks in here. Did someone step in a meadow muffin?

meaner than a junkyard dog---extremely mean or aggressive

I'd avoid her if I were you. She's meaner than a junkyard dog.

MeeMaw---great grandmother

MeeMaw's comin' for supper. I'd better start cookin'.

'member---"remember"

I still 'member when Len fell outta the china berry tree and landed on that barb wire fence.

mend one's fences--- to lay a dispute to rest; to forgive and make up after a dispute

I think you two should just quit bickerin' and mend your fences already.

menfolk---men

All the menfolk got together and had a barn raisin'.

Meskan---"Mexican"

I learned to speak Spanish fluently growing up near the Meskan border.

mess---a large quantity

Sissy stirred up a mess of wasps and got stung all over.

methinks---pronounced "MEEthinks"; I think

Methinks I'mone have myself a beer.

Mexican strawberries---pinto beans

We're havin' fajitas and Mexican strawberries for supper.

middling---"so so"; average; mediocre

Doctor: *And how are you feeling today?*
Patient: *Oh, just middlin'.*

might could---might be able to

Daughter: *Pa, can you give me a ride to the mall?*
Pa: *Well, I reckon I might could do that.*

might ought---should

You might ought to roll your window up before it starts raining.

mighty---very

It's gettin' mighty hot out here.

mighty white of you---
very kind of you.

Buddy: *Take some of that Bar-B-Q home with you.* Betty: *Why thank you. That's mighty white of you.*

mind---to obey

You kids best mind your mother or I'll get my belt!

mind you---remember, pay attention, be cautious

It's o.k. to swim in the crick, but mind you, there's lots of snakes.

mind your p's and q's---
"stay out of trouble",
to behave

You kids best mind your p's and q's while you're at your grandmother's.

minner---pronunciation of "minnow"

I caught the biggest fish of my life with just a little ol' minner.

mint julep---traditional Southern drink of mint tea with whiskey

We went to New Orleans in search of a mint julep.

Miss---sometimes used before a female's first name whether she's married or not

Well, hello Miss Gloria! I haven't seen you in ages.

Mississippi Delta blues---
(see "Delta blues")

Nothin takes me home like pure Mississippi Delta blues.

Mississippi mud

Mississippi mud---A brownie-like desert covered with chocolate and marshmallow cream

My Momma makes the best Mississippi mud.

mite---a small degree

It's a mite humid today.

Momma---mother; commonly used by Southern adults as well as children

Don't you be talkin' bad about my Momma. I'll whup you good!

Momma didn't raise no fool---"don't take me for an idiot"

Hell no, I didn't forget the tickets. Momma didn't raise no fool!

month of Sundays--- a long time

I ain't seen you in a month of Sundays.

moon pie---a round confection with marshmallow filling common in the South

Momma gave me some money so I could buy me a coke and a moon pie.

moonshine---illegally distilled corn liquor

Back in the day, PaPa made a lot of money sellin' moonshine.

more better/mo' better--- better, better than

I did a lot of work on that truck. Now it runs a lot more better.

more than you can shake a stick at---an excessive quantity

My finances are in bad shape. I've got more bills than you can shake a stick at.

mosey---to stroll casually, to go; to walk

I'mone mosey on over to the barber and get my ears lowered.

mosquito hawk--- a harmless insect resembling a large mosquito

Junior: *Momma, there's a bug in my room!*
Momma: *Leave it alone. It's just a mosquito hawk.*

Mossyhorns---name for a trophy size deer that's presumably old enough to have moss growing on it's antlers

I saw ol' Mossyhorns this morning, but I just couldn't bring myself to shoot him.

mostest---the most (see also "-est")

Thar musta been 'bout fifty deer standin' thar in that clearin'. That was the mostest I'd ever seen in one place.

motor---an engine

Mom blew the motor in dad's truck. Boy is he gonna be pissed!

mountain dew---corn liquor

Grandpa's been hittin' the mountain dew again.

much obliged--- "thank you", indebted

Thanks for your help. I'm much obliged.

mud bugs---crawfish (see "crawfish")

I've seen people suck down mud bugs like it was an Olympic event.

mud dauber---(see "dirt dauber")

We got three storage sheds and two of 'em's full of mud daubers.

muddin'---driving any offroad vehicle wildly through a mud bog for fun

We're goin' muddin' down in the bottom on Leroy's property. Wanna come along?

muggy---very hot and humid

It's always muggy down in Houston.

muscadine---a large grape common in the South

Would you be so kind as to pour me a glass of that muscadine wine?

My dogs are barkin'--- "My feet hurt"

Man, my dog's are barkin'. I'm not movin' for the rest of the day.

~N~

nary---none, not

He's got nary a lick of sense.

naw---no

Martha: *Did you eat the last piece of pie?*
Truman: *Naw. Wasn't me.*

nearabout---about; around; approximately

I guess it was nearabout 10:30 when I got home last night.

necked---naked

Hey Bessie, let's send the kids to your sister's house and get necked!

neck of the woods---geographical area, part of town

So what brings you to this neck of the woods?

necktie party/necktie social---a public hanging

We ain't had a good necktie social in over fifty years.

neither here nor there---irrelevant

What he does for a livin' is neither here nor there. I don't want any Yankee datin' my daughter!

neither hide nor hair---no indication of

He just took off and I've seen neither hide nor hair of him in three months.

nervous as a long-tailed cat in a room full of rockin' chairs---extremely nervous

Every time I have to go to the doctor, I get nervous as a long-tailed cat in a room full of rockin' chairs.

neutral ground---the concrete or grassy median between the two sides of a highway or divided road; the area where trolley cars run such as in New Orleans

You boys run down to the store and fetch me some flour and eggs. And be careful crossin' the neutral ground!

newfangled---newly fashioned, modern

My grandpa says that newfangled clothes are gaudy.

nigger---historically, a derogatory reference to an African-American, but also used to refer to a contemptible character of any race

(The use of this term is often considered offensive.)

nigger-rig---to improperly repair something just enough to work temporarily; may be considered offensive

My throttle broke in the middle of nowhere and I had to nigger-rig it to get home.

nigger-shooter---a slingshot; may be considered offensive

I got a whippin' 'cause I shot a car with my nigger-shooter.

nigger toes---Brazil nuts; may be considered offensive

There's beer in the fridge and a bowl of nigger toes on the coffee table. Help yourself.

nigh on to---almost, about, nearly

It was nigh on to thirty years ago, but I remember it as if it were yesterday.

ninny---1) a breast

Remember that Christmas when Aunt Ester got drunk and started showin' off her ninnies?

2) "sissy", a weakling, a whining person

You damn ninny! I've never seen anyone so afraid of the dark in all my life!

no account/no 'count---worthless

That no 'count bastard owes me money.

noggin---head

Skeeter fell out of a tree and landed on his noggin.

nohow---no way, anyway, besides

It don't matter to me nohow.

no more shame than a naked whore on a bedquilt---no sense of guilt or modesty

Damn it Ethel, put some clothes on! You got no more shame than a naked whore on a bedquilt!

none---at all; a common double negative

It don't hurt my feelin's none.

none too---not at all

Pa's none too happy about me scratchin' his truck.

nope---no

Harley: *Have you seen the Sheriff?*
Huck: *Nope, not today.*

N'Orluns/N'awlins--- common pronunciations of "New Orleans"

It's not hard to have a good time in N'Orluns.

norther---a cold front from the arctic usually accompanied by rain, sleet, hail, or snow

I need to wrap the pipes. There's a norther comin'.

no-see-ums---tiny insects

Momma says she hates campin' 'cause of the no-see-ums.

nothin' but a thang---no big deal

A little rain don't bother me. It ain't nothin' but a thang.

no use beatin' a dead horse---proverb meaning it's futile to attempt to change something that cannot be changed

So you got fired. Move on. There's no use beatin' a a dead horse.

nowadays---presently; in the current time frame as opposed to the past

We used to get our water from a well, but nowadays we have runnin' water.

'n' them---"and them"; people closely associated with the named person, usually family; pronounced "inEM"

I can't remember the last time I saw Leroy 'n' them.

nuculer---pronounced "NOOKyuhler"; nuclear

Grandpa thinks nuculer power is just a myth.

~O~

offen/off'n---off (of)

I broke my leg last year when I fell offen my deer stand.

okey-dokey---"o.k.", agreed

If you'll go clean your room, I'll make you some cookies. Okey-dokey?

Okie---a person born, raised, or living in Oklahoma

I've got lots of coon ass relatives, but not a single Okie in the bunch.

Oklahoma rain--- a dust storm

An Oklahoma rain blew in and scratched the hell out of my car.

okra---vegetable usually sliced and served boiled, pickled, or batter fried

I could make a meal of fried okra alone!

ol'---"old"; often used before someone's name even when that person is not old

It looks like ol' Leroy's late for work again.

old biddy---a cranky old woman

I'll be damned if I'm gonna invite that old biddy to Thanksgivin' dinner.

ol' boy---any male person; not necessarily old or a boy

That ol' boy never could manage to keep a job.

---

olden---old

We couldn't afford shoes back in the olden days.

older than dirt---very old

My grandpa is older than dirt.

old fogie---a prudish or old-fashioned person

My dad's an old fogie. He won't let me date until I'm eighteen.

old lady---wife or girlfriend

My ol' lady is constantly bitchin' at me fer leavin' the toilet seat up.

old man---1) husband or boyfriend

My ol' man is goin' huntin' this weekend.

2) father

Ask your ol' man if you can borrow his truck.

Old Man River/Old Muddy/Old Blackwater---nicknames for the Mississippi river

I once lost a boat to Ol' Blackwater.

Old Scratch---Satan, the Devil

That boy is so mean I'd swear he was the son of Old Scratch.

old-timey---old-fashioned

Hey, I see you've got one of them old-timey sepia pictures.

on account of---because

Mom says we have to walk home from school on account of she's too drunk to come pick us up.

---

once in a blue moon---
rarely, seldomly

I only get sick once in a blue moon.

open up a can of whoop ass---to assault someone, to become violent

If he don't watch his mouth, I'm gonna open up a can of whoop ass.

open up a can of worms---
to instigate a conflict or negative situation

Don't say anything about Uncle Leroy's girlfriend. You might open up a can of worms.

ornery---mean, stubborn, aggressive

I'll sell you my horse for cheap. She's too ornery for me to handle.

ought not---should not

Little boys that can't behave ought not go to the carnival with the good little boys.

oughtn't---
(see "ought not")

You oughtn't go swimmin'. It's fixin' to rain.

outen/out'n---out of

She came a runnin' outen the barn hollerin', "Snake! Snake!".

outhouse---a toilet located outside and away from the main house

Pa, get a gun! Thar's a snake in the outhouse!

out like Lottie's eye---
  1) unconscious, asleep

Boy, you sure whooped him good. He's out like Lottie's eye!

  2) outdated, out of style

Poodle skirts and bobby socks are out like Lottie's eye.

out of kilter/off kilter---
  misaligned, maladjusted,
  malfunctioning

Ethel hit a curb in my car and knocked my suspension off kilter.

out of whack---
  (see "out of kilter")

I haven't tuned that guitar in years. I'm sure it's all out of whack.

over yonder---
  (see "yonder")

Go fetch a bucket of water from the well over yonder.

~P~

pack---to carry

I walked across Texas packin' nothin' but the clothes on my back.

pallet---bedding comprised of blankets on the floor

Of course you can stay here tonight. I'll make you a pallet in the living room.

Palmetto State---nickname for South Carolina

I've got some relatives livin' in Charleston. That's in the Palmetto State.

panhandle---the northeastern extremities of the states of Florida, Oklahoma, and Texas

I once lost a good dog to a tornado out in the Texas panhandle.

PaPa/PawPaw/PeePaw--- grandfather or great grandfather

PaPa never did believe in spankin' the young'uns.

parish---a county in Louisiana

Land is mighty expensive in my parish.

partner---person to whom you are referring

Barkeep: *What can I get fer ya, partner?*

parts---a particular geographic area

We don't see too many Yankees in these parts.

pass by---to stop by

I'll pass by your house sometime this afternoon.

passel---a significant amount

My Granny's got a passel of cows.

Paw---father

My Paw done taught me everything he knew about fishin'.

pay no mind---ignore

Pay no mind to your brother. He's just teasing you.

peach---a pretty or likeable girl

You'll really like my niece. She's a peach.

peach fuzz---facial hair on a newly pubescent male

Little Joe's growin' up fast! He's already interested in girls and I think I even saw a little peach fuzz.

Peach State---nickname for Georgia

If ya can't deal with hurricanes, ya sure don't want to live in the Peach State.

peachy---1) fine, excellent

Joe Bob: *How are you doin' today?*
Bobby Joe: *Well, I'm just peachy! How 'bout you?*

2) terrible (sarcastically)

Joe Bob: *I accidentally dropped your fishin' pole in the bayou.*
Bobby Joe: *Oh, well isn't that just peachy!*

peachy keen---fine;
of good quality

That sure is a peachy keen little car you got there.

peaked---sickly

Are you feeling alright? You look a little peaked.

peart/pert---well, alert

At the ripe old age of seventy-five, I'm just as peart as I've ever been.

peart off---
to rebel verbally

Iffen you peart off to me one more time, I'm gonna tan yer hide!

pea shooter---a small gun such as a BB gun or a pellet gun

Let's go shoot us some cans with my new pea shooter.

pecan candy---candy made from pecans and sugar

My Dad makes the best pecan candy this side of the Mississippi.

pecker---a penis

Little boys are fascinated with their peckers.

peckerwood---woodpecker

Those damn peckerwoods are destroyin' my barn!

peecan---a common pronunciation of "pecan"

Granny's got a peecan tree in her back yard.

Pelican State---nickname for Louisiana

Every now and then, we get to go gamblin' over in the Pelican State.

pepper-belly---1) someone who enjoys hot or spicy food

I've always been a pepper-belly. I can eat jalapeños 'til the cows come home.

2) a derogatory reference to a Hispanic person

(The use of this term is often considered offensive.)

pert near---almost, close to

Supper's pert near done. Y'all go get washed up.

pert near, but not plumb---almost, but not quite

Sister: *Are you done in the bathroom?*
Brother: *Pert near, but not plumb. I'll be out in a minute.*

petered out---expended, exhausted

Somebody get some wood. The fire's almost petered out.

pick a fight---to antagonize to the point of violence; to initiate a fight or confrontation

He's been tryin' to pick a fight with me all day, and I've just about had it.

pick 'em up truck---(see "pickup")

I just bought me a brand new pick 'em up truck.

pickin' (at)---teasing

Don't get mad. I'm just pickin' at you.

pickle---a bind; a dilemma

My car broke down on the way to work and left me in a pickle.

pick one's brain---
to discuss something with someone; to get someone's opinion

Ya got a minute? I need to pick your brain about a few things.

pickup---a truck

I got rear-ended by a pickup this mornin'.

piddle/piddlin'---
1) goofing off, wasting time

It's time to go to school. Quit piddlin' and get ready.

2) to urinate

That damn dog piddled on my shoes again!

piddly ass---insignificant, scrawny, miniscule

I'm tired of workin' my fingers to the bone for a little ol' piddly ass paycheck!

pie-anner---humorous pronunciation of "piano"

I once had an upright pie-anner.

piece---a short distance

Let's walk down this trail a piece.

pill bug---
(see "doodlebug")

Sissy quit playin' with pill bugs the day she got that one stuck up her nose.

pine for---to yearn for

For years now, Bobby's been pinin' for Ellie, but she still won't give him the time of day.

pine knot---a piece of dead pine in which the sap has turned to turpentine; makes a good fire starter

Go fetch a pine knot and I'll build us a fire.

piney woods---thick forest; backwoods

Y'all be careful runnin' around out thar in the piney woods. Ya hear?

piss ant---a weak or spineless person

You piss ant! Stand up for yourself once in a while.

piss ass---weak or insignificant

That's the most piss ass excuse I've ever heard.

pisser---1) a toilet; a bathroom

Leroy: *Where's Bubba?*
Quincy: *He went to the pisser.*

2) misfortune

The game got rained out. What a pisser!

pissin' and moanin'---complaining

We're almost there so quit yer pissin' and moanin'.

pissin' in the wind---doing something futile

You're pissin' in the wind tryin' to start a fire with wet wood.

piss poor---bad, of poor quality

Leave me alone! I'm in a piss poor mood.

piss up a rope---sarcastic command for someone to go away

Why don't you go piss up a rope?

playin' possum--- pretending to be dead or asleep

Billy doesn't want to go to the dentist. He's in his room playin' possum.

plumb---completely

Aunt Mildred has gone senile. Yep, she's just plumb crazy!

plumb numb---drunk

Can you carry me home? I'm plumb numb.

podunk---of poor quality, substandard, worthless, tacky

That was the most podunk restaurant I've ever eaten at.

poke---a bag

Watcha got in the poke?

pole cat---a skunk

I can't seem to keep the pole cats out of my trash.

polk---greens served fried, usually with scrambled eggs and bacon

Momma's cookin' polk and eggs for breakfast.

polk, roll, and grits--- "nothing"; sarcastic reply to someone inquiring about a meal; short for "Poke your feet under the table, roll your eyes, and grit your teeth."

Son: *What's for dinner?* Pa: *Polk, roll, and grits if you don't finish your chores!*

polk salad---a heaping bowl of polk greens

You best eat all your polk salad iffen you want to grow up to be big and strong.

ponder on---to think about; to contemplate, consider

Linda: *What are you starin' at?*
Lenard: *Nothing. I was just ponderin' on goin' fishin' tomorrow.*

pooped---tired, exhausted

I just woke up and I'm pooped already!

poor boy/po' boy--- a submarine sandwich

Would you pick us up a couple of po' boys on yer way home from work?

pop---a carbonated drink

You got any pop in the fridge?

pop a squat--- (see "cop a squat")

Pop a quat and stay awhile.

porch baby---a child too young to venture past the porch

I remember when you were just a porch baby wettin' yer drawers.

posse---a search group; a lynch mob

When that feller broke out of jail, we gathered up a posse to go look for him.

powerful---extremely

It's powerful hot and you look powerful thirsty. Why don't you sit down and I'll fix you a cold drink.

pow-wow---a get together, a discussion, a meeting, a party

We're havin' a pow-wow at my house tonight, if y'all wanna come.

praline---a sugar coated pecan

Would you like a praline with your coffee?

preserves---homemade jam, typically preserved in mason jars

Mom makes the best apricot preserves.

pretty---very, significantly

It's pretty humid today.

pretty damn---excessively

It got pretty damn cold last winter.

pretty penny---a large sum of money

By the size of that diamond, I'd say that ring cost a pretty penny.

prit near---
(see "pert near")

It's prit near Christmas. Do you have all your shoppin' done?

probly/prolly---
common pronunciations of "probably"

I told Willie to pick up a loaf of bread, but he'll prolly forget.

pronto---(Spanish) immediately

My wife just went into labor. We need to get to the hospital pronto!

punkin---1) alternate pronunciation of "pumpkin"

They's havin' a punkin carvin' contest over at the community center.

2) a term of endearment

Come here, Punkin, and give Momma a kiss.

pup---a child

Feels like only yesterday, I was just a pup.

purdy/purty---pretty

That sunset shore is purty!

put one's tit in the ringer---to punish, to scold

That boy is three hours late. I'm gonna put his tit in the ringer when he shows up!

put one under the jail---said of someone deserving serious punishment

If that boy don't change his ways, they're gonna put him under the jail.

put on the back burner---to postpone

I don't have time to do it right now. I'll just have to put it on the back burner until I get around to it.

put out---upset; imposed upon

I reckon I'll stay for supper iffen I'm not puttin' you out.

put the hurt on---to cause harm to or punish someone

If I find out who shot my horse, I'm gonna put the hurt on 'em!

~Q~

queer as a three dollar bill---very strange; blatantly homosexual

I tell ya, that boy's queer as a three dollar bill. Next thing ya know, he'll be showin' up to work in a dress.

quicker 'n shit---very fast; "quicker than shit"

Throw yer line right over yonder, and I guarantee you'll catch a fish quicker 'n shit!

quietus---death; an end to something

Behave or I'll put a quietus on you!

quilled---a pronunciation of "coiled"

I found a snake quilled up in the chicken coop!

quiltin' bee---a gathering for the purpose of knitting quilts

Are you goin' to the next church quiltin' bee?

~R~

rabbit ears---
  a television antenna

Will you adjust the rabbit ears while you're up?

racket---excessively loud,
  or alarming noise

You kids knock off all that racket! Momma's tryin' to watch her stories.

**rainin' like a cow pissin'
on a flat rock**---raining
heavily

Jethro: *Is it still rainin' outside?*
Leroy: *Like a cow pissin' on a flat rock!*

raised in a barn---lacking
  the proper mannerism of
  closing a door behind
  oneself; used as an insult

Go back and close that door. Were you raised in a barn?

raisin' cane---
  (see "raisin' hell")

The dogs are raisin' cane in the front yard again. Will you go see what they're barkin' at?

raisin' hell---1) engaging
  in a disruptive argument
  or confrontation

If you don't quit raisin' hell with the neighbors, somebody's gonna call the police.

2) celebrating

I'm gettin' married tomorrow, so I'll be raisin' hell tonight!

rambunctious---unruly, reckless, hyper

Why did I have to be cursed with the most rambunctious kids on Earth?

rampy---tasting of garlic or wild onions

This is good soup, but it's just a bit too rampy.

rarin' to---enthusiastic and ready

I'm all gussied up and rarin' to go!

rash of shit---a scolding

The last time I came home late from the bar, my wife gave me a rash of shit.

rat killin'---chores, duties; what one was previously doing

Well, I reckon I ought to get back to my rat killin'.

RC---Royal Crown cola; a quintessential Southern beverage

Would you like somethin' to drink? I've got RC, tea, orange juice, and beer.

read up---familiar with, knowledgeable

I ain't read up on that subject, but we could talk about bait worms.

reckon---to think, to reason, to suppose

Well, it's after midnight. I reckon I should go to bed.

recollect---remember

Man, I just can't recollect what I did with my keys.

red beans---kidney beans

Can you pick up some red beans and rice while you're out?

red beans and rice---
a standard Creole
side dish

Southern fried chicken is often served with red beans and rice.

red bugs---(see "chiggers")

Last time Ma went campin', she got into a mess of red bugs and hasn't gone back since.

red-eye? (you)---
"Are you ready?"

Bubba: *It's time to go. You red-eye?*
Willie: *Ready as I'll ever be.*

red light---a traffic signal

I got in a wreck down at the red light.

redneck---a poor, white,
resourceful, rural, working
class, Southerner; usually
implies ignorance or lack
of education; sometimes
considered offensive

A redneck in a pick-up truck helped me pull my car out of the mud.

revival---a lively religious
event

A revival is about the most fun you could ever have in church.

ribbin'---teasing, joking
with

Aw, don't get mad. I'm just ribbin' ya.

rig---an 18 wheel cargo
truck

I'd like to own my own rig someday.

right---very; downright
(see "downright")

I'm right parched. Got any lemonade?

right directly---promptly

Waitress: *I'll be back right directly with your drinks.*

right in the head---sane; of sound mind

Aunt Bessie ain't quite right in the head.

right purty---very pretty

It's a right purty day today!

right quick---quickly, for just a minute

C'mere right quick. I want to show you something.

right then and there--- at that precise moment

I remember the first time I saw her. I couldn't help but fall in love with her right then and there.

riled up---excited, angry

Don't get the dog all riled up. She'll piss all over herself.

ripe---rotten, foul smelling

Whew! You are ripe! Go take a shower!

road apple--- (see "meadow muffin")

I'd hate to be the guy in the parade who has to pick up the road apples.

rode hard and put up wet---"used and abused"; very unattractive

You couldn't pay me to date your sister. She looks like she's been rode hard and put up wet.

rot gut---cheap liquor

Keep drinkin' that ol' rot gut and you'll be pushin' up daisies in no time.

rough-housin'--- sparring or playing recklessly

Y'all quit rough-housin' in the livin' room.

rubbed off (on)--- influenced

I spent a week in Louisiana and the dialect rubbed off on me.

ruckus---a noisy commotion

I heard a ruckus in the barn. Go check it out!

ruint---a pronunciation of "ruined"

My wife thought it was ok to shift gears without usin' the clutch and ruint my transmission.

run---to drive

Can somebody run me to the store?

runnin' like a sugar tree---flowing profusely

I cut my finger wide open and the blood started runnin' like a sugar tree.

runnin' off at the mouth/ runnin' one's mouth--- talking incessantly

I'll never take her out again. She's always runnin' off at the mouth.

rustle up---to find, gather, or prepare

Go rustle up some wood and I'll build us a fire.

ruther---a pronunciation of "rather"

I'd ruther be layin' on a beach somewhere.

rye-cheer---pronunciation of "right here"

I'm gonna sit rye-cheer and watch the football game.

sack---a bag

I've got a sack of peanuts. Want some?

sam hell---
 a mild expletive

What the sam hell are you doin'?

San Antone---
 San Antonio, Texas

It's a long haul from Memphis to San Antone.

sarsaparilla---root beer

Have you ever tasted home made sarsaparilla?

sass---
 verbal insubordination

You might sass me now, but wait until your father gets home from work.

savvy---to understand

Do you savvy what I'm tryin' to tell ya?

sawbuck---a $10 bill

Could you loan me a sawbuck 'til payday?

scalawag---a crook;
 a disreputable person

I can spot a scalawag a mile away.

scalded corn bread---
 corn bread batter mixed
 with scalding hot water
 and cooked in a greased
 iron skillet

Momma fixes scalded corn bread on Saturdays.

scare up---to locate

I think I'm gonna scare up something to eat. I'm kind of hungry.

scarf---to eat hastily

Don't scarf your food, son. You'll get a stomach ache.

scarf up on---to eat a substantial amount of

Don't scarf up on candy before supper. You'll ruin your appetite.

scat (cat)---1) command for a cat to go away

Scat! Get off my desk!

2) "bless you" after someone sneezes

schoolin'---education

You won't get anywhere in life without the proper schoolin'.

scuppernong--- the muskadine grape

That is some damn fine scuppernong wine!

see a man about a horse--- to use the restroom

Ooh, I'll be back. I need to see a man about a horse.

see fit---to believe to be appropriate

My parents seen fit to put me in military school on account of the public school done kicked me out.

seen---saw

I seen a wolf up on the ridge!

**See you later alligator.
Afterwhile crocodile.**---
a common exchange of
farewell

Guest: *It's been nice seeing
you. See you later alligator!*
Host: *Afterwhile crocodile!*

set---sit

*Set still and finish your
supper.*

shack up---to live with an
intimate partner to whom
you are not married

*Have you heard about
Bessie Lou shackin' up
with Earl?*

shade tree---a large tree
providing plenty of shade

*We should have the cook-
out at your house because
you have more shade trees.*

shade tree mechanic---
a novice mechanic;
only works on an
automobile if absolutely
necessary

Withrow: *Do you know
anything about rebuilding
a carburetor?*
David: *Nope, I'm just a
shade tree mechanic.*

**shakin' like a dog shittin'
peach pits**---shaking
uncontrollably

*That haunted house scared
Becky so bad she came out
shakin' like a dog shittin'
peach pits.*

sharp---1) of high quality;
pleasing to the eye

*Well don't you look sharp!
Is that a new suit?*

2) intelligent, witty, clever

That boy is sharp, I tell ya.

shat---past tense of "shit"

*Goddamn it! The dog shat
on the rug again!*

shenanigans---acts of mischief

I will not tolerate any shenanigans in my house!

shindig---any celebration, particularly a party or dance

I'm havin' a shindig this weekend and y'all are all invited.

shining one's belt buckle---dancing

Wilbur's been shinin' his belt buckle all night long.

shiner---a black eye

Who gave you that shiner?

shinny---climb

Shinny up that tree and see where we are.

shin oak---a small tree or bush

I tore my leg up on a shin oak. I knew I should have worn jeans.

shiteater---a dog; pronounced "shiTEEter"

I got a good shiteater. He'll fetch ducks and everythang!

shitfire---a general exclamation

Well, shitfire! I ain't seen you in a coon's age.

shit from shinolah---nothing

Billy don't know shit from shinolah!

shit hemorrhage---a fit, a tantrum

We'll get to the airport on time. Don't have a shit hemorrhage!

shit no!---no (emphatically)

Johnny: *You didn't lose that lottery ticket, did you?* Bubba: *Shit no! Are you nuts?*

shit on a shingle---toast topped with a ground beef gravy

Do y'all want sandwiches or shit on a shingle for dinner?

shit or get off the pot--- "hurry up and take action or get out of the way"

Shit or get off the pot! I don't have all day to wait on you.

shittin'---bluffing, joking

Courtney: *Are you shittin' me?*
Damon: *I wouldn't shit you. You're my favorite turd.*

shitter---a toilet; a bathroom

Sis: *Where's Dad?*
Bro: *I think he's in the shitter.*

shittin' and gittin'--- doing something with haste

We were shittin' and gittin' because we were already four hours behind.

shitty---1) drunk

I tend to get pretty shitty during the holidays.

2) of poor quality

This is the shittiest pizza I've ever eaten!

3) rude

Hey, don't get shitty with me. I'll kick your ass!

shoddy---of poor quality, malfunctioning

Their service is so shoddy, I wouldn't let my dawg eat at that restaurant!

Shoog---short for "Sugar" a term of endearment (see "Sugar")

I'd do anything for you, Shoog!

shoot---1) "ask me"

Daughter: *Daddy, I have a question.*
Dad: *Shoot.*

2) euphemism for "shit"

Aw shoot! I broke a nail.

shootin' iron---a gun

I bought me a new shootin' iron. Wanna see it?

shoot the shit---to talk

I just thought I'd stop by to shoot the shit with ya.

shore/sho'---pronunciations of "sure"

It shore is mighty hot!

shotgun---the front passenger seat in an automobile

I've got shotgun on the way to the beach.

shotgun shack---a narrow house with the rooms arranged in a line from front to back

Uncle Jeb finally sold that ol' shotgun shack and moved off to the country.

shotgun wedding---a forced wedding; insinuates that the father of the bride is holding the groom at gunpoint

I heard Cletus got Annie Mae pregnant. I predict there will be a shotgun wedding in his future.

show---a movie theater;
  a movie

*We're all goin' to the show.
Wanna come?*

shuck---to remove the
  shells from oysters or
  the husks from corn

*Growin' up on a farm will
make you hate shuckin'
corn.*

shucks---"gosh", "golly"

Shucks, I'm speechless.

shut-eye---sleep

*Y'all be quiet! I'm trying to
get some shut-eye.*

sick to one's stomach---
  nauseated

*Creamed corn makes me
sick to my stomach.*

simmer down---command
  for one to calm down or
  be quiet

*Simmer down before you
say something you'll regret.*

sinch ya's---since you are

*Sinch ya's already up, will
you grab me a beer?*

sippin' whiskey---high
  quality whiskey, not to
  be wasted

*Slow down! That thar's
sippin' whiskey.*

sitcheeayted---humorous
  pronunciation of
  "situated"

*I just moved into a new
house. It'll be weeks before
I get fully sitcheeayted.*

sittin' pretty---to be in a
  secure or prosperous state

*Ol' Leroy is sittin' pretty
since he got his inheritance.*

six-gun---
  (see "six-shooter")

*He came runnin' out of the
bar with six-guns a blazin'.*

six-shooter---a six-shot revolver

Wanna see my new six-shooter?

skedaddle---to leave in a hurry

You're gonna be late if you don't skedaddle.

skeered---a pronunciation of "scared"

I'll race any car in town. I ain't skeered.

skeeter---a mosquito

Close the door! You're lettin' the skeeters in.

skin---to punish harshly

I'm gonna skin ya if you ever do that again!

skippin' rock---a smooth, flat rock suitable for "skipping" across the surface of a body of water

Doc's boy hit Boudreaux's boy in the head with a skippin' rock and now they's a feudin' like hillbillies.

skittish---nervous, easily frightened

My dawg's gettin' skittish in her old age.

skivvies---underwear

The doctor will be in shortly. Go ahead and strip down to your skivvies.

slew---a large quantity

There's a slew of beer in the fridge. Feel free to help yourself.

slack-jawwed---dumb; ignorant; mentally slow

I'll be glad when she comes to her senses and stops datin' that slack-jawwed boy from Arkansas.

slim and none---a small chance or poor odds that something will happen

Chances are slim and none that I'll ever become President.

slim pickin's---an inadequate selection to choose from

Looks like we got slim pickin's in the pantry. Y'all wanna go out to eat?

slop---1) left-over food fed to pigs

Be sure to scrape your plate into the slop bucket!

2) to feed pigs

Did you remember to slop the pigs this mornin'?

slow as molasses---extremely slow

Will you hurry up! I swear, you're slow as molasses.

slow time---standard time (i.e. the opposite of Daylight Savings Time)

I just can't get used to this slow time.

smack dab---directly centered

Willard went to a baseball game and got hit right smack dab in the head by a foul ball.

small taters---an insignificant matter or situation

I wouldn't worry about it if I were you. Sounds like small taters to me.

smart as a box of rocks---dumb or ignorant

Don't listen to anything she says. She's about as smart as a box of rocks.

smart off---
(see "peart off")

Don't you smart off to me! I'll slap you into next Tuesday.

smarts---1) intelligence, know-how

It takes a lot of smarts to be a chemist.

2) stings, hurts

Ooh, that smarts. That's the last time I walk in front of a pitchin' machine.

smell good---cologne or perfume

Can I borrow some smell good? I've got a date.

smidgen---
a small quantity

I think the chicken needs a smidgen of salt.

s'mores---a delicious desert comprised of campfire roasted jumbo marshmallows sandwiched with chocolate between two graham crackers

My favorite part of campin' is makin' s'mores after dinner.

snap---reason, awareness

You've got to appear in court in 10 minutes. Where's your snap?

snap beans---green beans; string beans

Grandma used to make us peel buckets upon buckets of snap beans.

snipe huntin'---a prank where the victim is left in the woods, in the dark, holding a bag, "huntin' snipe" (see "huntin' snipe")

Remember when we took Bubba snipe huntin'? It took him 45 minutes to get back to camp.

snot-slingin' drunk---
extremely intoxicated

Whoo, boy! I got snot-slingin' drunk last night!

snug as a bug in a rug---
warm, cozy, comfortable

This lodge is cozy. I feel snug as a bug in a rug.

soam bitch---pronunciation of "son of a bitch"

That soam bitch stole my horse!

social---a dance or party

I met the girl of my dreams last night at the social.

soda (sody) pop---any sweet carbonated beverage

I'm out of orange juice, but I've got plenty of soda pop. Want one?

soda (sody) water---
(see "soda pop")

I need to go to the store for more soda water. Do you need anything?

so dry the trees are bribin' the dogs---
extremely dry due to a lack of rain

It hasn't rained in weeks. It's so dry the trees are bribin' the dogs!

so mad I could spit---
very angry

Boy, sometimes you just make me so mad I could spit!

some odd---an undefined amount

We must've driven a hundred and some odd miles before we came to a gas station.

somethin' fierce---with gusto; adds emphasis to a statement

Pull over here. I've gotta piss somethin' fierce!

son---any male to whom you are speaking

Damn, son! That's a hell of a sunburn!

son of a biscuit eater---euphemism for "son of a bitch"

Son of a biscuit eater! I'm late for work.

son of the South---any Southern male with Southern virtues

No son of the South would ever tolerate someone talkin' bad about his mama.

sooie---word used to call swine

SOOIE! Come and get it pigs!

Sooner---a resident or native of Oklahoma

I've never, nor will I ever, be a Sooner.

sop---to soak up

Don't waste that gravy. Sop it up with your biscuit.

Southern cross---the Confederate battle flag, a long time icon of the South

I get all teary-eyed every time I see the Southern cross.

Southern drawl---the slow, Southern manner of speaking; the southern accent

Foghorn Leghorn had a heavy Southern drawl.

Southern fried---cooked in the Southern style by breading and frying

Southern fried chicken and mashed potatoes are standard at any Southern truckstop.

Southern hospitality--- exceptional hospitality

No matter where you go, you just can't beat that Southern hospitality.

Southland (the)--- The South; equivalent of "homeland"

It's been 20 long years since I've seen the Southland.

Southron---old spelling and pronunciation of "Southern"

Momma wants me to marry a decent, hard-workin', Southron boy.

sparrow grass--- alternate pronunciation of "asparagus"

Mom, can I have some more sparrow grass?

speak your piece--- to speak one's mind, to speak freely, to get something off one's chest

Well, you've got my attention. Go ahead and speak your piece.

spell---1) a short period of time

Take yer shoes off and set a spell.

2) temporary illness or disorientation

Ma went to lay down. She's havin' a spell.

spiffy---of good quality, nice looking

Those sure are some spiffy shoes.

spittin' image---
a strong resemblance;
a near replica

You are absolutely the spittin' image of your Daddy!

s'posin'---pronunciation
of "supposing"

S'posin' I do help you. What's in it for me?

spraddle---
(see "spread-eagle")

Don't sit spraddle, dear. It's unbecoming.

spread-eagle---having
one's legs spread apart

It ain't fittin' for a woman to sit spread-eagle.

spring chicken---a youth;
exhibiting youthful
qualities

Well you know, Dear, you ain't no spring chicken anymore.

squander---to waste,
to disperse foolishly

My wife's down at the mall squanderin' my money.

squarsh---1) pronunciation
of "squash" (vegetable)

Eat your squarsh. It's good for you.

2) to crush

The kids are out back squarshin' bugs in the flower bed.

squat---nothing

I didn't get squat for a Christmas bonus this year.

squaw---a female

Hey man, check out the squaw at the bar.

squeeze box---
an accordion

I use to play the squeeze box, but nowadays, I'm a bit rusty.

squirrelly---silly

Get it out of your system now. I don't want you actin' squirrelly at your sister's wedding.

staggerin' around like a blind dog in a meat house---to be lost in euphoria

Bubba's got it bad for Annie Mae. Anytime she enters the room, he starts staggerin' around like a blind dog in a meathouse.

Stars and Bars---the flag of the Confederacy

Grandpa flew the Stars and Bars over his house for years.

stay---reside

Where do you stay at these days?

step-ins---panties

Be sure to pack extra step-ins for your stay at grandma's house.

steppin' over dollars to pick up dimes---blindly passing up a good thing for second best

I don't know why she ever broke up with him. She's just steppin' over dollars to pick up dimes!

stick in the mud---a pessimist; a stubborn, negative person

Pete: *I don't want to go. I hate bar-B-Q.*
James: *You don't have to like bar-B-Q to have fun at the chili cook off. Don't be such a stick in the mud!*

sticks in one's craw---said of something upsetting or bothersome

My vacation got postponed. That really sticks in my craw!

sticks to your ribs---said of food that is very filling

Mom's cookin' sure does stick to your ribs!

stitch---any article of clothing

She got drunk and before you knew it, she was runnin' through the house without a stitch on.

stone's throw---a short distance

Wanna go down to the swimmin' hole? It's just a stone's throw up the road.

stop light---a traffic signal

Yankee: *Can you tell me where the RV lot is?*
Cooter: *Go thataways and turn left at the third stoplight.*

story---a lie

You're not tellin' me a story are ya?

straight from the horse's mouth---directly from the original source

Flo: *Where did you ever hear such a thing?*
Beth: *I heard it straight from the horse's mouth.*

Stretch---a name for a tall, skinny person

Hey Stretch, how's the weather up there?

stretched---sick, ill

I've been stretched for a week and I still don't feel any better.

stubborn as a cross-eyed mule---extremely stubborn and ornery

I just can't get that boy to eat his vegetables. He's about as stubborn as a cross-eyed mule.

study on---to ponder; to consider

I been studyin' on takin' a vacation, but I don't think I can afford it.

suckin' heads--- the practice of sucking the fat and juice out of the head of a boiled crawfish (see "crawfish")

Aunt Linda liked suckin' heads until the day she inhaled one and had to be rushed to the hospital.

suckin' the hind tit--- said of a victim of misfortune

My girlfriend ran off with my best friend and left me here suckin' the hind tit.

sugar---1) a kiss, kisses

Come give your Granny some sugar.

2) term of endearment

Anything for you, Sugar.

sugar britches---a term of endearment

Good night, Sugar britches.

sum bitch---a common pronunciation of "son of a bitch"

That sum bitch stole my truck!

sump'n---a common pronunciation of "something"

Mom, can I have sump'n to drink?

Sunday-go-to-meetin'---
church worthy; of good
quality

Go put on your Sunday-go-to-meetin' clothes. We're goin' to get yer picture made.

Sunshine State---a
nickname for Florida

I think I'm gonna retire to the Sunshine State.

sun-up---daybreak

I want to be in the boat and on the water by sun-up.

supper---the evening
meal, as opposed to
"dinner"

I invited my boss over for supper on Friday.

sure as I'm standin'
here---positively,
absolutely, definitely

JD: *I know a girl who got hit by lightnin'.*
Dave: *Really?*
JD: *Sure as I'm standin' here.*

sure as shit---positively,
guaranteed

That dog loves to hunt. You shoot a duck, and sure as shit, he'll bring it to you.

Sure enough?/Sho 'nuff---
"Is that so?"; "Really?"

PaPa: *Says here in the newspaper that ol' Willie Nelson's in some kind of trouble with the IRS.*
MaMa: *Oh? Sure enough?*

swaller---1) a single
mouthful of a beverage

I know he's only three but one swaller of beer ain't gone hurt him.

2) pronunciation of
"swallow"

Yuck! I think I swallered a fly!

swamp dew---moonshine

Grandpa's out in the barn cookin' up some swamp dew.

swawmp---common pronunciation of "swamp"

You boys stay out of the swawmp. There's gators out there.

sweatin' like a whore in church---sweating profusely

Damn it's hot! I'm sweatin' like a whore in church.

sweet as a Georgia peach---likeable, pretty, polite

I sure would like to date that gal. She's just as sweet as a Georgia peach!

sweet enough to rot your teeth---said of a very nice or beautiful female

You're damn lucky to have that girl. She's sweet enough to rot your teeth.

sweet gum---sap extracted from a sweet gum tree, as chewing gum

I haven't had sweet gum since I was a little kid on the farm.

Sweetie pie---a term of endearment

Sweetie pie, could you fix me a drink?

sweet on---to have amorous feelings for

If I didn't know better, I'd say you were sweet on me.

sweet potato---a yam

Every Thanksgivin' Momma cooks sweet potatoes covered in marshmallow cream.

sweet potato pie---
pie made from yams

I'm bringin' a sweet potato pie to the pot luck dinner.

sweet talk---1) to charm
or flatter

Maybe you can sweet talk her into goin' out with you.

2) flattery

That sweet talk might work on some girls, but it won't work on me!

sweet tea---tea sweetened
with sugar

I'll have some sweet tea and a piece of blackberry cobbler.

swig---1) a single mouthful
of a beverage

Take a swig of this and tell me what you think.

2) to drink

Go ahead, swig it on down.

swill---to drink quickly

I been sittin' around swillin' beer all day. And Ma says I ain't persistent.

swimmin' hole---a deep
spot in a creek suitable
for swimming

Momma come quick! Bubba got bit by a snake down by the swimmin' hole!

switch---A thin, green
branch or twig

Momma whipped me with a switch for not comin' straight home from school.

~T~

tacky---gaudy, distasteful

Mildred wore the tackiest dress to the funeral.

tailgate party---a gathering outside where people park their trucks together and sit on the tailgates; usually in a parking lot on the main drag in a city or perhaps at a beach; also common in the parking lots of stadiums before or after a sporting event or concert

I heard the police broke up the tailgate party after the concert last weekend.

t'ain't---there isn't; it isn't

T'ain't nothin' a little love cain't cure.

take after someone--- to display similar character traits as someone

If that boy takes after his father, he won't amount to anything.

take a long walk off a short pier---an insulting command for someone to go away

Ya know, I've had just about enough of your mouth. Why don't you go take a long walk off a short pier.

take a shine to---to develop a liking for

Looks like the dawg took a shine to your leg.

take down a notch---
  to humble someone;
  to punish

Willy kept shootin' his mouth off until someone finally took him down a notch.

take leave of one's senses---to become irrational, illogical, or out of control

I think she took leave of her senses when she started datin' that feller.

take to---to accept or befriend

She took to him like she had known him forever.

take too kindly to---to be accepting or forgiving; to welcome

We don't take too kindly to horse thieves around here.

take to the bank---to believe in something; to rely on something; take as the given truth

No daughter of mine is datin' until she's sixteen and you can take that to the bank!

take up for---to defend

I would always take up for my sister, no matter what the circumstances.

talk a cow out of her calf---to negotiate well; to be very persuasive

Martha is one hell of a saleswoman. She could talk a cow out of her calf.

talk atcha later---
  "talk to you later"

Mom: *Call me if you need anything.*
Son: *Alright. I'll talk atcha later.*

talleywhacker---a juvenile word for "penis"

A boy really learns about pain the first time gets his talleywhacker caught in his zipper.

tan one's hide--- to give one a spanking; to punish or assault

I'm gonna tan your hide iffen you're not home on time for dinner.

tarnation---a euphemism for "damnation"

What in tarnation is your problem?

tarred---a common pronunciation of "tired"

I'm sick and tarred of workin' my fingers to the bone!

ta ta's---"breasts"; may be considered offensive

What a lovely pair of ta ta's you have.

taters---short for "potatoes"

Ma punished me by making me peel taters all day.

tearin' up the pea patch--- behaving wildly and unruly; misbehaving

I have to go to the store and I don't want y'all tearin' up the pea patch while I'm gone.

teeniney---very small; combination of the words "teeny" and "tiny"

For such a teeniney person, you sure got a big mouth.

tenny-runners---tennis shoes; athletic shoes

I ran so much last week, I wore out my tenny-runners.

Tex-Mex---the spicy, Texas version of Mexican food

I'm starvin'. Let's go get some Tex-Mex. I'm hungry.

Texas pinstripe---tobacco spit out the window of a moving vehicle and smeared down the side

I'll let you borrow my truck if you promise not to leave any Texas pinstripes.

thang---a common pronunciation of "thing"

Hand me that thang over there.

thankee---"thank you"

Thankee, ma'am. I really appreciate your help.

thank you much--- "thank you very much"

Joe: *This is the best pie I've ever had!*
Courtney: *Well, thank you much. I made it myself.*

thar---a common pronunciation of "there"

I musta stood thar in that line for over thirty minutes.

That dog will/won't hunt--- "That will/won't work."

Kid: *Did I tie my shoes right, Pa?*
Dad: *Yep. That dog'll hunt.*

That'll learn ya---"That will teach you a lesson"

Millard: *I hit my head on the coffee table.*
Willard: *Well, that'll learn ya not to wrestle in the house.*

That's how the cow eats the cabbage

That's how the cow eats the cabbage.---"That's the undeniable truth"

I don't like it either, but unfortunately, that's how the cow eats the cabbage.

that there---that

That there is the purtiest gal I ever did see.

the big city--- any metropolitan area

Pa's goin' to the big city to get the car fixed.

the Big Easy---the city of New Orleans

Ever been to the Big Easy?

the bug---a contagious illness

I feel terrible. I think I've got the bug.

the country---a rural area away from metropolitan areas

My grandmother's got some land out in the country.

the crud---an illness; the common cold

Timmy can't play outside today. He's got the crud.

the evil eye--- a disconcerting stare

My momma's always givin' me the evil eye.

the house---my, our, or your house

We're headed to the house if y'all want to come by.

the Law---the police; law enforcement personnel

We have to turn the music down. Someone called the Law.

them---those

Them flowers you got out front sure are purty!

them's fightin' words---
"what you've said could
incite someone to become
violent"

Jethro: *Your woman's
lookin' mighty fine.*
Cletus: *Watch it now!*
Them's fightin' words!

them there---those

*Hand me them there
matches so I can light
the stove.*

**There's more than one
way to skin a cat**---
"there are other ways
to solve a problem"

*My ride left without me,
but I'll get home somehow.
There's more than one way
to skin a cat.*

these here---these

*These here grapes sure are
mighty sour.*

**the shit's gonna hit the
fan**---"there will be
an argument, a fight,
or a confrontation"

*The shit's gonna hit the fan
when your wife finds out
you quit your job.*

**the short end of the
stick**---a negative
outcome, a loss

*In one day, I lost my job, my
wife, and my wallet. Once
again, I ended up with
the short end of the stick.*

the whammy---a hex, a
curse, a spell

*That old lady's plum crazy!
She thinks someone put
the whammy on her.*

the whole enchilada---the
object(s) spoken of, as a
whole

*I went to the casino with
$5000 and lost the whole
enchilada.*

they all---they

They all went down to the rodeo without me.

they's---1) they are

Your parents called and said they's comin' over around seven.

2) there is

They's no time like the present.

they-uns---they

They-uns won't be here for another week.

thingamabob---a name for an object used in lieu of it's proper label

Do you have any of those thingamabobs for holding corn on the cob?

thingamajig--- (see "thingamabob")

What do you call that thingamajig that hangs from the back of your mouth?

thinks the Sun come up just to hear him/her crow---said of someone who is vain or conceited

She's so stuck up she thinks the Sun come up just to hear her crow!

thin skinned---said of someone who cannot endure the slightest ridicule

Don't get mad. I was only kiddin'. You shouldn't be so thin skinned.

This ain't my first rodeo--- "I've been around", "I've done this before", "I know what I'm doing"

Ed: *Are you sure you know what you're doin'?* Earl: *Hey now, this ain't my first rodeo.*

thisaways/thataways---
this way; that way

He was so drunk, he couldn't stand up. He kept leanin' thisaways and thataways until he just fell over and passed out.

this here---this

This here pie is pretty tasty.

through the grapevine---
by word of mouth; gossip

I heard, through the grapevine, that you're gonna get married.

throwed---1) confused

That riddle throwed me, but I finally figured it out.

2) threw

I throwed Leroy out of my house fer insultin' my wife.

ticked (off)---angry

Dad's ticked off 'cause Mom wrecked the car.

tickled (to death)---to be very happy or amused

My daughter is fixin' to get married and I'm just tickled to death about it.

tie a not in one's tail---
to impede; to punish

That boy's two hours late. I'm gonna tie a not in his tail when he shows up.

tighter than a mare's ass at fly time---
1) excessively thrifty

I haven't gotten a raise in three years. My boss is tighter than a mare's ass at fly time!

2) extremely tight

Can you open this jar for me? The lid's on tighter than a mare's ass at fly time!

'til the cows come home---
for a long time;
indefinately

Son, you can bitch 'til the cows come home, but you still have to eat all your vegetables.

tizzy---a fit, a tantrum

Don't get yourself in a tizzy. I'll take you to the carnival.

toad floater/strangler---
(see "turd floater")

Hurry home from school. The weather man said there's a toad floater a comin'.

toadfrog---a toad or a
frog

We dissected a toadfrog in Biology class today.

**to have a burr under
one's saddle**---to be
agitated, aggravated,
irritated, angry

Be on your toes. The boss has got a burr under his saddle.

**to have/put one's ass
in a sling**---to punish;
to be punished

Dad'll have my ass in a sling iffen I'm not home on time for supper.

to have the misery in the head---to be clumsy, scrawny, or weak

Poor ol' Bessie never was much good at sports. She's got the misery in the head, you know.

to-kill-ya---a humorous pronunciation of "tequila"

We drank to-kill-ya all night long and now I've got a horrible hangover.

tomfoolery---mischief

You boys settle down. I won't have none of that tomfoolery in my house!

tommy toes--- small tomatoes; cherry tomatoes

I don't want any tommy toes in my salad.

too big for one's britches--- proud to a fault; "cocky" insubordinate

You're gettin' too big for your britches. Go to your room!

took ill---became sick

Bessie took ill last month. Doc says she ain't gonna make it.

too pooped to pucker--- extremely tired

I've been workin' all day and now I'm too pooped to pucker.

tore up---1) very upset

Our best milkin' cow died yesterday. Ma's all tore up about it.

2) extremely intoxicated

I've seen you drunk plenty of times, but you were tore up last night!

to send packin'---to end a relationship or to evict someone from a property

Ellie's deadbeat boyfriend wouldn't get a job so she finally sent him packin'.

to speak of---worth mentioning

Cooter ain't got no friends to speak of, unless you count his dog.

tote---to carry

Willy came in totin' a case of beer.

to the gills---overwhelmed; to the maximum; more than enough

I can never seem to get my readin' done. I'm up to the gills in books.

t'other--- "the other"

It don't make no differ'nce one way or t'other.

to think one hung the moon (and stars)---to hold someone in the highest regard

As far as she's concerned, he can do no wrong. She thinks he hung the moon.

to turn yellow---to become frightened or nervous

That dog come a barkin' and Leon turned yellow.

towhead---a blonde-haired person

Melba was born a towhead, but eventually it turned red.

trailer trash--- a derogatory reference to someone who lives in a trailer or anyone with a low standard of living or lack of class; may be considered offensive

Momma, Joey said we were trailer trash. Are we trash, Momma?

trashy---disreputable; in a state of disrepair

I don't want you hangin' out with trashy people like that! You hear?

tromp---to stomp; to walk heavy-footed; to trample

Why do you kids insist on trompin' through the mud?

trot line---a length of fishing line with baited leader hooks at regular intervals along it's length and suspended in the water with buoys; used to catch fish, usually catfish

Fire up the boat. We gotta go pull in the trot lines.

tuckered out---tired, exhausted

You kids have got me plumb tuckered out.

tump---to spill or knock over

I tumped over a glass of juice and stained the carpet.

turblanche---white sand or rock; an area where white rock gullies havebeen created by erosion

Go out to the turblanche and tell your brother to come home for dinner.

turd floater---a storm; a heavy rain

There's a turd floater comin'. Go roll up the car windows.

turkey fuck---a negative situation; a predicament

Well this turned into a real turkey fuck! This is the last time I drive anywhere without a spare.

turned around---lost

Sorry it took us so long to get here. We got turned around in Mississippi.

turn loose---to let go; to release a grasp on something

Turn loose of your sister before I tan your hide.

twang---1) a zestful flavor

That picante sauce sure has got some twang to it.

2) a thin, metallic musical sound or timbre

I really love the twang of a Southern guitar.

'tweren't---"it wasn't"

Beth: *Thanks for mowin' my yard.*
Billy: *'Tweren't nothin'.*

~U~

ugly---mean

Now don't be ugly to your sister, Billy.

umpteen---an undefined numerical amount

I've asked for a raise umpteen times and still haven't gotten a dime.

unlessen---unless

I'm not drivin' that far unlessen you're payin' for the gas.

up air---pronunciation of "up there"

I heard you went to Alaska. What'd you go up air fer?

up and---suddenly

That ol' boy lived on the farm for thirty years until one day he just up and moved to the city.

up a storm--- "with a passion"

Saturday night we kicked off our shoes and danced up a storm.

upbringin'---raised with the proper education of etiquette, morals, and manners

Boy, get your elbows off the table. Didn't you have no upbringin'?

upchuck---to vomit

He got sick during the meeting and upchucked on the Vice President.

171

up shit creek

up shit creek (without a paddle/with a turd for a paddle)---to be in a situation with no possible good outcome

You're gonna be up shit creek without a paddle when your wife finds out you wrecked her car.

up under---underneath

Crawl up under the truck and see if you can tell where the oil leak is.

used to could---"was once able to"

I can't drink 'til the mornin' light like I used to could.

useless as tits on a boar---of no use whatsoever

I'm gonna have to fire that guy. He's about as useless as tits on a boar.

~V~

Vaminose---alternate pronunciation of the Spanish "Vamos", "let's go"; command for one to leave

Vaminose! I'm tired of lookin' at ya.

Vamoose--- (see "Vaminose")

We need to vamoose. It's a long drive home, and I have to go to work in the morning.

varmint---a form of "vermin"; animals, usually small and undesireable

I been sittin' on the porch all day, shootin' varmints out of my garden.

veranda---a covered porch

My wife wants me to put a swing out on the veranda.

Virginny---the state of Virginia

Back in Virginny we used to dance all night 'till the Sun come up!

visitin'---conversing; talking

You're not interrupting anything. We were just sittin' here visitin'.

vittles---food

I need to stop at the store and pick up some vittles for supper.

voodoo---Creole form of black magic; witchcraft

To this day, my great grandmother still practices voodoo.

~W~

walkin' on a slant---drunk; intoxicated

Boy I was walkin' on a slant last Saturday! I tell you what!

walkin' stick---a praying mantis

I caught a walkin' stick on the window screen.

waller---pronunciation of "wallow"; to roll around in something

You're filthy! Have you been wallerin' in the mud all day?

warsh---pronunciation of "wash"

Can I warsh my clothes at your house?

warsher---a washing machine

Go take the clothes outta the warsher and put 'em in the dryer.

warshin' powders--- laundry detergent

On your way home, stop and pick me up some warshin' powders so I can warsh the clothes.

wash---a place where water has flowed across a dirt road, partially eroding it

If that wash gets any bigger, we won't be able to drive to town.

washette---a laundromat

My dryer is broken. Can you give me a ride to the washette?

waterin' hole---a bar

I'm goin' down to the waterin' hole to drown my sorrows.

wear out---to destroy by excessive use

You'll wear out the seat of your pants if you sit on your ass all the time.

wear out one's welcome--- to overstay one's welcome; to become unwelcome

Your brother has got to go. He's worn out his welcome.

wear the britches---to be the dominant partner in a relationship

Make no mistake, Mildred wears the britches in that house.

wear you out---tire you; spank you, assault you

Boy, you're tryin' my patience. I'm fixin' to wear you out.

Wee (Woo) dogie--- "Man oh man"; "Goodness gracious"

Weeeee dogie! It's mighty hot!

we've howdied but we ain't shook---"we've met but barely know each other"

Host: *Do you know Beth?* Guest: *Yes. That is, we've howdied but we ain't shook.*

Well, button my britches--- (see "I'll be damned")

Well, button my britches! What on Earth are you doin' here?

Well, I'll be---short for "Well, I'll be damned."; a general expression of surprise, wonder, disbelief, frustration, etc. (see "I'll be damned")

Well, I'll be! I've never seen a pair of eyes quite as pretty as yours.

well hell---"well, anyway"; "then again"

Well hell, I guess I'll call it a night and go on home.

Well, shut my mouth--- (see "I'll be damned")

Well, shut my mouth! I just can't believe she would ever do such a thing.

went---"leave"

Let's went. We're already runnin' late.

went to shit and the hogs ate him/her---sarcastic reply to an inquiry as to someone's whereabouts

Mother: *Do you know where you're brother ran off to?*
Daughter: *He went to shit and the hogs ate him.*

went to town---indulged in something wholeheartedly

Damn, you must've been hungry. You went to town on that hamburger!

we-uns---we

What we-uns want is the right to bear arms!

weren't---wasn't

What'd you say? I weren't listenin'.

wet back---a derogatory reference to a Mexican or Hispanic person

(The use of this term is often considered offensive.)

wet behind the ears--- inexperienced, naïve

I shouldn't have hired that guy. He's still wet behind the ears.

wet one's whistle--- to wet one's mouth; to drink something

You ought to wet your whistle with some of Grandma's lemonade.

whar---a common
pronunciation of "where"

Whar'd you ever heard such a thing?

whar 'bouts?---a request
for more specific
information in regards
to location

Whar 'bouts did you say you shot that deer?

What can I do ya fer?---
"How can I be of
service to you?"

Store clerk: *Howdy! What can I do ya fer?*
Customer: *Gimme a pack of Winstons and a Slurpee.*

Whatcha know good?---
"How are you?";
"What's new?"

I ain't seen y'all in years. Whatcha know good?

what on Earth---
"what" emphasized

What on Earth are you doin' up at this hour?

**Where (have) you been
hidin'?**---"Where have
you been and what have
you been doing since I
last saw you?"

Hey, Leroy. Long time, no see. Where you been hidin'?

whilst---while

Looks like Santa Claus done come whilst y'all were sleepin'.

whippersnapper---
a strong, healthy youth

I was ten foot tall and bullet-proof when I was a young whippersnapper.

whippin'---a spanking

Boy, you're on my last nerve and you're fixin' to get a whippin'.

whistlin' Dixie---bluffing, joking; lying; (see "You ain't just whistlin' Dixie)

You kids go clean your rooms. Right now! I ain't whistlin' Dixie.

white lightnin'--- moonshine liquor

I've been savin' this bottle of white lightnin' for a special occasion such as this.

white trash---a derogatory reference to a Caucasian person

(The use of this term is often considered offensive.)

whitewash---1) a cheap white paint

Son, go down to the store and pick up a gallon of whitewash.

2) to paint something with whitewash

I'll pay you five dollars to whitewash the garden fence.

whitey---a derogatory reference to a Caucasian person

(The use of this term is often considered offensive.)

whole hog--- whole-heartedly

Bubba wants to win this watermelon eatin' contest. He's goin' after it whole hog.

whole shebang---
everything collectively,
as a whole

The IRS took my house, my car, and the whole shebang.

whoop/whup---to beat or
assault; to spank

He thought he could push me around, but I whupped him good!

why for---"why";
"for what reason"

Why for you do that to me?

widow maker---a dead tree
branch that falls suddenly

A widow maker fell on my dawg. I'm sure gonna miss her.

will do---"I will do that";
an acknowledgment

Sis: *Gimme a holler when you get back in town.*
Bro: *Alrighty. Will do.*

winder---a pronunciation
of "window"

Hey man, why don't you roll up that there winder? I'm freezin'.

wired---finished, solved,
fixed

I've almost got it wired. Just a few more pieces and this puzzle is finished.

wishbone---a 'y' shaped
bone found in fowl that,
when broken between
two people, is believed
to grant a wish to the
holder of the longer piece

Who wants to split the wishbone with me? Anyone?

woant---a common pronunciation of "want"

What do y'all reckon you woant for supper?

wolf---to consume hastily

That boy acts like he ain't eaten in 10 years! Did you see the way he wolfed that food down?

womenfolk---women

It ain't fittin' to be tellin' dirty jokes around the womenfolk.

Wonder State---a nickname for Arkansas

She's from Arkansas, and you know what they say about people from the Wonder State.

won't amount to a hill of beans--- "won't amount to anything"; "won't affect anything"

Without perseverance, you won't amount to a hill of beans.

woods---forest

Don't wander off into the woods. You'll get lost.

wore out---worn out, exhausted

I've been workin' all day and I'm plumb wore out.

wormy---nervous, hyper

I can't stand wormy little dogs.

~Y~

Ya hear?---"Do you understand?"; "Are you listening?"

You'd better write me a letter every now and then. Ya hear?

yahoo---any unexceptional person; implies ignorance or low social standing

Emma ran off with some yahoo from Nebraska.

y'all---"you all"; you (plural)

Are y'all comin' down for Thanksgivin'?

y'all come---"you all come back and see me again"

Millard: We'll see you next time.
Willard: Bye now. Y'all come!

y'all come back now--- (see "y'all come"); does not mean "now", but rather sometime in the future

See y'all later. Y'all come back now, ya hear?

y'all'r---"you all are"

Y'all'r gonna have to move y'all's car.

y'all's--- belonging to you all

Y'all's house is a lot bigger than mine.

Yank---(see "Yankee")

Pa always said, "The only good Yank is a dead Yank!"

Yankee

Yankee---a person born, raised, or living in the Northeastern U.S.; generally regarded by Southerners as being rude and intolerable

I've only met one Yankee that I could tolerate and he was a mute.

Yankee shot--- an old term for "navel"

I have no idea what possessed my daughter to get her Yankee shot pierced.

Yankeeville---the northeastern U.S., particularly New York City

I have to go to Yankeeville for a three day business trip. That's three days too long.

yay---a description of size usually indicated with one's hands

You shoulda seen the fish I caught last week. It was about yay big and weighed 38 pounds!

yee-haw---1) an explosive vocalization of merriment or excitement

Yeeeeeeeee–haaaaaaaaaw! I love this roller-coaster!

2) sarcastic expression of a lack of enthusiasm

Ma: *Your Great Aunt Mildred is coming to visit for a while.*
Bubba: *Well, yee-haw.*

yeller--- 1) a common pronunciation of "yellow"

You watch out for them yellerjackets. They'll sting the fire outta ya.

2) scared

What's the matter, Gus? You ain't yeller, are ya?

yellow-belly---a coward; cowardly

Come out and fight like a man, you yellow-belly son of a bitch!

yep---yes

Father: *Have you seen my keys?*
Son: *Yep. They're on the coffee table.*

yer---your; you're

Can I marry yer daughter?

Yes'm---"Yes ma'am" (see "ma'am")

Ester: *You are just a growin' like a weed!*
Billy: *Yes'm! I eats my vegetables.*

yes-sir-ee(-bob)---yes, absolutely

Bartender: *Would you like another drink?*
Bar fly: *Yes-sir-ee-bob! I do believe I would!*

yokel---a country person; one accustomed to life in the country; implies slow mentality or low social standing

People up North think we're all just a bunch of dumb yokels.

yonder---area "over there" to which speaker is referring

Ma: *Billy, have you seen yer sister?*
Billy: *Yep. She's yonder by the fenceline.*

y'oant---pronunciation of "(do) you want"

We're goin' fishin'. You can come along if y'oant to. Well, y'oant to?

You ain't just whistlin' Dixie---"You speak truthfully"; "You're not kidding"; "I agree with you completely"; (see "whistlin' Dixie")

Ma: *That is one fine sunset.*
Pa: *You ain't just whistlin' Dixie!*

you all---you (plural) (see "y'all")

Are you all comin' down for Christmas this year?

you best--- "you had better"

You best hurry up or you'll miss the bus.

you'll catch more flies with honey than you will with vinegar--- proverb meaning that one can get what one wants faster through niceties than through force

I told her I was sorry, and to my surprise, she bought me dinner. It just goes to show, you'll catch more flies with honey than you will with vinegar!

you must not be holdin' your mouth right---"You must be doing something wrong."

Eileen: *I can't get my car to start.*
Irma: *Well, you must not be holdin' your mouth right.*

young buck---a youth, a child

Last time I seen you, you was just a young buck.

young'uns---children

I'm takin' the young'uns to the movies.

your druthers is my ruthers---"Your preference is fine with me."

Adam: *Can we just stay home and order pizza?*
Eve: *Of course. Your druthers is my ruthers.*

your go---your turn

Pay attention to the game. It's your go.

yourn---belonging to you

This one is mine and that one is yourn.

you talk about---expression used to add emphasis to a statement

I shot myself in the foot once. You talk about pain! I thought I was gonna die.

you'uns---you (singular or plural)

You'uns go on in the house and get washed up for supper.

~Z~

zilcher---a stick wrapped with plastic (milk jug, cellophane, etc.) on one end, and held over a fire until the plastic melts and drips producing a "zipping" sound

Some of my fondest memories are of sittin' around campfires makin' zilchers.

Zydeco---a Cajun style of music emphasizing the accordion and fiddle

No crawfish boil would be complete without some loud Zydeco music.

SOUTHERN TONGUE

A Dictionary of Southern Expressions

Complete the order form below and send it along with your check or money order for the appropriate amount to:

Nomad Publishing, P.O. Box 244722,
Anchorage, AK 99524

Southern Tongue: $11.95 per copy

**Shipping and handling: $3 for first book,
$2 for each additional copy**

Quantity: _____ @ $11.95 each = _____

Shipping and handling = _____

Total = _____

Ship to:

Name: _____

Address: _____

City: _____ State: ___ Zip: _____

Phone: _____

E-mail: _____

SOUTHERN TONGUE

A Dictionary of Southern Expressions

Complete the order form below and send it along with your check or money order for the appropriate amount to:

Nomad Publishing, P.O. Box 244722,
Anchorage, AK 99524

Southern Tongue: $11.95 per copy

Shipping and handling: $3 for first book,
** $2 for each additional copy**

Quantity: _____ @ $11.95 each = _____

Shipping and handling = _____

Total = _____

Ship to:

    Name: _____

    Address: _____

    City: _____ State: ___ Zip: _____

    Phone: _____

    E-mail: _____

Southern Tongue

A Dictionary of Southern Expressions

Complete the order form below and send it along with your check or money order for the appropriate amount to:

Nomad Publishing, P.O. Box 244722,
Anchorage, AK 99524

Southern Tongue: $11.95 per copy

Shipping and handling: $3 for first book,
                               $2 for each additional copy

Quantity: _____   @ $11.95 each = _____

Shipping and handling = _____

Total = _____

Ship to:

Name: _____

Address: _____

City: _____ State: ___ Zip: _____

Phone: _____

E-mail: _____